# PORTRAIT OF CALVIN

PORTRAIT OF CALVIN

Published by Desiring God
P. O. Box 2901
Minneapolis, Minnesota 55402

Cover design and illustration by: Cory Godbey and Matt Mantooth at Portland Studios, Inc.

First Published and Printed, 1954, in Great Britain
by S.C.M Press, Ltd.

Printed in the United States of America

Parts of the original paragraphing have been altered to facilitate the book's easier reading fifty years later. Editorial additions by Desiring God have been bracketed.

# PORTRAIT OF CALVIN

by

**T.H.L. PARKER**

# TO THE TWO MARIES

**MARY ANGWIN,**
March 1, 1936

and

**MARY PARKER,**
June 14, 1940

*Love's not Time's fool*

# FOREWORD

An Appreciation for Calvin and His *Portrait*

JOHN PIPER

Desiring God is publishing T. H. L Parker's *Portrait of Calvin* out of theologically and historically informed nostalgia—and a sense of mission. The mission is to make much of the majesty of God. And the nostalgia is that this book was my first serious exposure to Calvin. I paid fifty cents for the book in a used rack. That was four decades ago.

Parker's *Portrait* was first published in 1954. But it's not the kind of book that goes out of date, because it's only trying to be current with the sixteenth century. If you get it right, it stays right. When I saw the 500th anniversary of Calvin's birth coming (July 10, 2009), I thought that maybe others would enjoy the same introduction to Calvin I enjoyed.

It may sound strange, but the main function Calvin has played in my life has been inspiration, not formation. My theology, which is Calvinistic, was formed along other lines, mainly in exegetical classes on Paul, then shaped by the depths and heights of John Owen and Jonathan Edwards. Doing exegesis forced me to take the text seriously. Owen wove the textual threads into rich tapestries. Edwards hung them on banners and rode them into the heavens.

Only later came a serious engagement with John Calvin. The brightness and magnitude of his vision of God was magnetic. Different from Edwards, Calvin is everywhere exegetical. Edwards is tethered to the text, but his cord is at times very long. Calvin did what Edwards never did: He wrote commentaries and preached hundreds of sermons covering whole books of the Bible.

So for me, Calvin became a great inspiration as a preacher. Unlike so many today, he really believed that preaching and exegesis and coherent theology go together. "Such preaching as this," Parker says, "pursued so regularly and applied so stringently to the people, was the central explosive point of the Church's work in Geneva" (95).

I am eager for people to know Calvin not because he was without flaws, or because he was the most influential theologian of the last 500 years (which he was), or because he shaped Western culture (which he did), but because he took the Bible so seriously, and because what he saw on every page was the majesty of God and the glory of Christ.

Calvin continues to inspire me because of his relentless focus on the greatness of God. He did not always have eyes for the majesty of God. His medieval training left him in spiritual darkness. Parker says that "he was taught to think in a room with the windows shut" (28). But then light dawned. "I saw—just as if light had broken in upon me—in what a pigsty of error I had wallowed, and how polluted and impure I had become" (34).

Not long after his move into the majesty of grace came his move from urban Paris to the majestic mountains of Geneva. "From the house there was a fine view over the lower town to the Jura Mountains on the left, the Alps on the right, and in the middle the Lake bordered by its vineyards and hills" (76). I do not doubt that such sights worked for Calvin the way Psalm 19 says they should—declaring the glory of God.

But Geneva was not a vacation. Calvin is inspiring because he labored among so much real life and accomplished so much against such great odds. "He was not unfamiliar with the sound of the mob outside his house threatening to throw him in the river and firing their muskets" (31). Trials were so many and so varied Calvin said, "This I can truly testify, that not a day passed in which I did not long for death ten times over. But as for leaving that Church to remove elsewhere, such a thought never came into my mind" (39).

We might think that such a setting would knock the wind out of a man's productivity. It was not a peaceful place to write. Parker reminds us, "It is strange to realize that for most of his life Calvin's house was full of young children [not his own]" (80). But Parker also observes that "Calvin was born to write" (47). Geneva could not cut off Calvin's creative productivity as a writer.

> He had inevitably less time to give to study and to the polishing of his sentences with the City Council worrying him about drains and heating apparatus, with ecclesiastical quarrels to settle with other Churches and worries and sickness in his own home. But, in fact, he could hardly have written so voluminously if he had been allowed his quiet life in Strassburg or Basel. (47)

"Even in his last illness he only stopped dictating about eight hours before he died, his voice at last playing him traitor" (81). Calvin's writings, including the famous *Institutes of the Christian Religion*, were "not written in an ivory tower, but against the background of teething troubles" (80).

Nevertheless, "in the definitive edition of his works, the *Corpus Reformatorum*, his writings fill forty-eight quarto volumes printed in double column" (47). And amazingly, this writing proves helpful again and again. "We shall time and time again be struck dumb with admiration at his transparent ease when dealing with even the most abstruse problems" (57).

If you wonder where to begin reading, Parker suggests the commentaries: "I would suggest that the *Commentary on St. John's Gospel* makes a good introduction to Calvin, and after that one might go on to the *Commentary on Ephesians*" (59).

Calvin kept his focus. The simplicity of his life and friendship is inspiring. His life had no frills. "Here in the Rue des Chanoines Calvin lived very simply. . . . At one time he asked for his salary to be reduced to bring it into line with that of his colleagues, but the Council would not hear of it. It is enough to say that he lived without financial worry, but he did not get rich at Geneva's expense" (77-78).

In all this simplicity and labor, he made friends and kept them. Parker says, "He had a way of making and keeping friends. . . . People knew just where they stood with him. Deceit was utterly foreign to his nature. . . . It was just because he was unswerving in his devotion to God that he was such a good friend" (84).

In the end, Calvin's manifold ways of inspiring us have the effect they do century after century because he saw the gospel so clearly and made Christ so central. Here is his summary of the center of the gospel and what we must tell a man when we preach:

> that he was alienated from God by sin, an heir of wrath, liable to the punishment of eternal death, excluded from all hope of salvation, a total stranger to the blessing of God, a slave to Satan, a captive under the yoke of sin, and, in a word, condemned to and already involved in, a horrible destruction; that, in this situation, Christ interposed as an intercessor; that He has taken upon Himself and suffered the punishment which by the righteous judgment of God impended over all sinners; that by His blood He has expiated those crimes which make them odious to

God; that by this expiation God the Father has been duly satisfied and atoned; that by this intercessor His wrath has been appeased; that this is the foundation of peace between God and men; and that this is the bone of His benevolence towards them. (70)

If Jesus Christ, in all his majesty and excellence, is kept in clear view, the church will be kept from many errors. Therefore, Calvin continues to inspire and serve the church five hundred years after his birth. As Parker emphasizes in this inspiring "portrait," keeping Christ in clear view was John Calvin's "theological program" (66). He cites this passage from Calvin's *Commentary on Colossians*:

> For how comes it that we are "carried about with so many strange doctrines" (Hebrews 13:9), but because the excellence of Christ is not perceived by us? . . . This, therefore, is the only means of retaining, as well as restoring, pure doctrine: to place Christ before the view such as He is with all His blessings, that His excellence may be truly perceived. (66)

I pray that for all his imperfections Calvin will continue to have these inspiring effects: the disciplined submission to Scripture, the exaltation of the majesty of God, the unwavering commitment to expositional preaching, the full-orbed proclamation of the gospel, and the steadfast focus on the excellence of Christ.

John Piper
Minneapolis, Minnesota
December 23, 2008

# PREFACE TO THE
# DESIRING GOD EDITION

When I was asked to write a life of Calvin for the S.C.M. Religious Book Club, there were reasons why I was happy to agree. For one thing, it offered a pleasant relief from the arduous task of translating Karl Barth's *Kirkliche Dogmatik* into English, which had taken up much of 1950 and 1951. More importantly, there had been no biography of Calvin for many years. Moreover, I saw this as an opportunity to correct some of the commonly held misunderstandings and prejudices clustered around his name.

Yet I was not unaware of the particular difficulties confronting me in my extensive parish in the deep fens of Lincolnshire. Biographers require facts, and the facts can, for long dead figures, only be gathered from books. But the Cambridge University Library lay some seventy miles away and could be visited only infrequently. My solution of the difficulty was to treat the proposed work, less as a piece of scientific history than as my own view or interpretation of such facts as seemed relevant to Calvin's life and works. In other words, I would, like a portrait painter, look at my sitter and depict as faithfully as I could what I saw. Thus it became *Portrait of Calvin*. (But here I must emphasize that this book cannot stand as a rival to my later *John Calvin: A Biography* [1975]. The two are related, of course, as having a common subject and a common author. But there the relationship should cease.)

Now, what do I at the age of ninety-two make of this book that I wrote in 1952 and 1953 in my mid-thirties? It would be strange and unnatural if there were not a few things that I would now either say differently or not say at all. None of these affects the substance. It is not, of course, for me to praise or blame the work. We may leave that to the reviewers. Far more important is the subject of the portrait. After writing several books about Calvin, translating some others and editing not a few, I have not at all changed my mind about the heart of the matter, which may be found on pages 56 and 61 of this Desiring God edition. Calvin states his adherence to the witness of the Old and New Testaments to Jesus Christ: "This, therefore, is the only means of retaining, as well as restoring, pure doctrine:

to place Christ before the view such as He is with all His blessings, that His excellence may be truly perceived."

By his faithfulness to this confession, all Calvin's work stands or falls.

T.H.L. Parker
December 13, 2008

# CONTENTS

*Introduction*                                      *21*

I      The Training of a Reformer               25

II     The First Attempts                       39

III    Man of Letters                           47

IV     The Theologian                           61

V      Number Eleven, Rue des Chanoines         73

VI     Minister of the Word of God              85

VII    The Conflict of the Word                 97

VIII   The Ecumenical Churchman                111

       *Last Words*                            *127*

# INTRODUCTION

The number of books on Calvin seems endless.

On the [European] continent, the river has been high, if not in spate, most of the time since the celebrations in 1909 of the fourth centenary of his birth. Even in England, there has flowed a trickle sufficient for a man to wet his thirst. Why, then, yet another?

The great Emile Doumergue has surely told us all that can at present be known about the history of Calvin's life. And if we lack the time, patience, or French to make the Grand Tour of those seven huge volumes, we can still find out all we need to know from Mr. R.N. Carew Hunt's *Calvin*, which—whatever qualifications must be made about its interpretation of the Reformer's theology—is reliable and well-written history.

There is little point in entering into competition with Mr. Carew Hunt by putting forward another biography. But, because some village or other has been photographed from every possible angle, I am not prevented from attempting a watercolor of the same place. So the title of this book should be taken as differentiating it somewhat from a straight biography. It is a portrait, not a photograph.

The presentation may come, I hope, as a pleasant surprise to some who have always in their imaginations seen Calvin with horns and wreathed about with the incense of brimstone—those who, had they the organizing of Madame Tussaud's, would move his not very lifelike effigy from its present position in the Main Hall into the Chamber of Horrors. Perhaps I may be allowed two anecdotes to illustrate the irrational aversion against him among my brethren in the Church and also the popular ignorance of his position in church history.

A new clerical acquaintance and I were talking of John Knox. He was reminded of John Calvin.

"Calvin, now," he said, "he was terrible."

"Terrible," I asked, "how?"

"I mean Calvin," he said, "you know about Calvin, don't you?"

He plainly thought I had not caught the name. Calvin was terrible. No one, surely, who called himself a loyal Anglican could dissent from the verdict that Calvin was terrible.

"But why terrible?" I asked.

He found the question difficult. It was axiomatic that Calvin was terrible. But in what way, it was not easy to say, especially if one knew of him only by hearsay. But he was a strong-minded man and refused to be beaten.

"He was terrible," he replied firmly. And then, with inspiration, "I mean, look how bad-tempered he was."

Then there was the man in an evening class. Romans 3:21 and following was being expounded. The teaching of the Council of Trent was mentioned and also that of Luther and Calvin. He interrupted me at the name: "Calvin," he said, "he was all on about predestination, wasn't he?"

Bad temper and predestination! A gruesome picture, certainly, but rather too bad to be true. Nobody could be quite so bad as that. But let it not be inferred from what we have just said that we intend to make Calvin better than in fact he was. Othello left the cardinal rule for all biographers:

> *Speak of me as I am; nothing extenuate,*
> *Nor set down aught in malice.*

Besides, Doumergue used up all the whitewash when he was busy redecorating Calvin, and there is none left for us. Nevertheless, the Calvin we see is neither angelically good nor diabolically evil. Alongside undeniable faults, we shall see undeniable virtues in him.

One fact will, however, stand out above all others—or rather, it will be the basic truth of his life. It is the essential harmony of the man. There are, of course, dissonances that spoil the harmony. But in spite of them, the last and truest thing to be said of Calvin is that, within the limits of sinful mortality, the unity of his life is astounding. His thoughts, his actions, and his intentions point in the same direction. As he thought, so he lived, and so he purposed. He was like an Old Testament prophet in that he proclaimed the Word of God both by words and by actions. In that sense, the course of his life takes on a certain sacramental reality. It bore visible witness to the gospel he preached. It is this harmony or consistency that gives its particular significance to Calvin's life.

CHAPTER 1

# THE TRAINING OF A REFORMER

For a hundred years and more, the magnificent structure of Church and common life that the Middle Ages had painfully built out of the ruins of the old Roman Empire had shown signs of wear. And, as will happen when buildings are not well looked after, time only accelerated the decay.

In theology, the universal breadth of the thought of Thomas Aquinas had given place to the "mummified philosophy" of the fifteenth century. The odor of decayed sanctity hung about the cloisters of the old monastic orders. And the enthusiasm of the poor brethren of St. Francis had grown something tarnished by the breath of the world. If this is only a general picture, with a vast deal to be said on the other side, it is nevertheless a generally true picture. It was not only the so-called "Reformers before the Reformation" who attacked the Church. Many of her most devoted and loyal children were the least sparing of her faults.

Yet the calls for reform met with little response from the Roman court. Here and there a little was put right, and here and there a little was made worse. A few bones were tossed to the dogs to stop their barking. But the radical reform of the Church was not attempted.

We may well doubt whether the Roman Church could have been reformed from within at this time. Certainly, she reformed herself in the Counter-Reformation of the sixteenth century, but not before she had been shocked into action by the widespread Protestant revolt.

In the most important respect, moreover, the calls for reform which came from within the Church differed in purpose from those of the Reformers. They had for their object the removing of practical abuses in organization, worship, and morals. So far as theology was concerned they were content to define what was already believed. But, for the Reformers, the reformation of doctrine stood in the forefront, and from it flowed all the other reforms which they attempted.

The Reformation was first and foremost a theological revival. Luther, Zwingli, and Calvin regarded their work as a bringing to light again of the great doctrines of the Scriptures, neglected or obscured by the medieval schoolmen.

Calvin himself had no hand in beginning the Reformation. He appeared late on the theological scene, when the early battles had been won and the Reformation was an established fact. By the time he was born in 1509, the monk Luther had spent four years of spiritual anguish and search after a peaceful conscience in his monastery. While he was still learning to read, Luther was already giving his evangelical lectures on the Psalms, Romans, and Galatians at Wittenberg. He was only a schoolboy when Luther took that step—a little step it seemed to him, not knowing that it was wearing seven-league boots—of publicly questioning the right of the papacy to levy indulgences.

Although all this was taking place as Calvin grew up, he was untouched by it. Everything in his upbringing combined in making a firm and zealous churchman of him.

His father was a lawyer to the Cathedral Chapter—something kin to a Diocesan Registrar in these days. In that house, the flavor was distinctly ecclesiastical. The many clerical visitors with their cathedral talk brought the family into a closer relationship to the Church than most laity enjoyed. What was more, the predominating atmosphere in his hometown of Noyon was ecclesiastical, and he grew up under the shadow of the Cathedral. This training and environment produced the desired effect, so that, looking back at his early life, he could say, "I was obstinately devoted to the superstitions of Popery."

From the time he was a small boy, the course of his life was determined. He was to take [holy] orders. In this he had the support of the Chapter, which defrayed some of the expenses of his education. He had his early schooling in the family of the de Montmors, patricians in Noyon. And here another strand was woven into the thread of his life and character, for with them he not only learned his grammar but also imbibed in aristocratic outlook that was to add a certain dignity to his demeanor throughout his life. Indeed, it must be confessed that this somewhat stiffened in him towards the end, so that he had not a little of the *grand seigneur* about him—as witness the incident in a Genevan street when a grateful but too enthusiastic refugee addressed him as "Brother Calvin" and was informed that the correct title was "Monsieur Calvin."

At fourteen, he departed with the two de Montmor sons and their cousin Claude de Hangest for the University of Paris. It was fitting, if somewhat ironical, that the great Reformed theologian should have his early training in the greatest medieval theological school. But the Paris of

ecclesiastical - relating to a church

the sixteenth century was no longer the glorious Paris of the spring and summer of the Middle Ages. There were no longer names like Albertus Magnus, Thomas Aquinas, or Peter Abelard to bring eager students flocking from the ends of Europe to her lecture rooms.

Paris was grown tired with age. Her theology lived in the past, not creatively but with a hardened traditionalism that made it irrationally suspicious of any fresh approach to a problem, let alone a new idea. The medieval undergraduate had ever been a riotous, careless creature, and his younger brother of the sixteenth century was probably not much worse, though conditions in Calvin's college, where Erasmus and Rabelais had spent unhappy years before him, were a scandal even in that age neither squeamish in manners nor over meticulous in morals.

At Paris, Calvin was at first an arts student, and at the Collège de la Marche had the good fortune to be taught Latin by one of greatest of all French schoolmasters, Mathurin Cordier. From him Calvin gained the mastery of Latin that was to make the Institutes one of the best written books of the Renaissance—Scaliger, the classical scholar, said that his Latin was almost too pure and elegant for a theologian.

Calvin acknowledged the debt he owed his old master when twenty-seven years later he dedicated to him the *Commentary on the First Epistle to the Thessalonians:*

> It is befitting that you should come in for a share in my labors, seeing that, having entered on a course of study under you, I became so far proficient as at least to be prepared to profit the Church of God in some degree. When my father sent me, still only a boy, to Paris after I had merely tasted the first elements of Latin, Providence so ordered it that for a short time I had the privilege of having you as my teacher, so that I might be taught by you the true method of learning, in such a way that I might be prepared afterwards to become somewhat more proficient. For after presiding over the first class with the highest renown, when you saw that pupils who had been ambitiously trained by the other masters produced nothing but show, nothing solid, so that they needed to be formed by you all over again, you grew tired of this nuisance, and that year descended to the fourth class. That indeed, was

your purpose, but to me it was a singular kindness on the part of God that I happened to have an auspicious beginning of such a course of training. And although I was permitted to have the use of it only for a short time, since soon afterwards we were advanced higher to a stupid man who regulated our studies according to his own pleasure, or rather caprice, yet I derived so much assistance afterwards from your training that I have good reason to acknowledge myself indebted to you for such progress as has since been made. And this I wanted to testify to posterity, that, if any advantage shall accrue to them from my writings, they shall know that it has in some degree originated from you.

From the general studies of the Collège de la Marche, he migrated to the Collège de Montaigu for his special theological course. Here he was taught the Nominalist theology which had long ruled supreme in Europe. His reading would be mainly in the schoolmen of the later Middle Ages with a few exceptions coming in from the halcyon days of medieval theology.

Duns Scotus and William Occam and Gabriel Biel from the fourteenth and fifteenth centuries would be his daily fare, and above all, the *Sentences* of Peter Lombard. No doubt he would make the acquaintance of the fathers, some of them—but it would be the fathers seen through the eyes of the Middle Ages. He was taught to think in a room with the windows shut—no breath of air came in from outside to disturb the atmosphere.

The Reformation was well on its way in Germany, where Luther was pouring out books and pamphlets. Even in France questions were being asked and dangerous answers given them. But none of this would disturb Calvin, wrestling with subtleties and hyper-subtleties of scholastic philosophy—unless perhaps it was mentioned by way of refutation.

But while Calvin is at Paris learning theology, his father and the Cathedral Chapter at Noyon have been getting at cross purposes. The trouble had nothing in it of religion and was simply a business matter. But it had the effect of making him dissatisfied with the clergy in his own town and no doubt also with the Church in general.

In this frame of mind, he decided that his son should not, after all, be a theologian but a lawyer. And besides that, he was not unaware from his own experience that the law "commonly raised those who followed it to wealth."

So Calvin's formal education in the Queen of the Sciences came to an end when he was nineteen. From Paris he had learned to read and write Latin. He was intimate with the Nominalist schoolmen, rather less so with the other main branch of the medieval tradition, the Realists, like Thomas Aquinas, and had read something of the fathers. He came to think little of the schoolmen in later years. He asked the Cardinal Sadoleto:

> Do you remember what kind of doctrine candidates for the ministry learned in the schools? You yourself know that it was mere sophistry, and sophistry so twisted, involved, tortuous and puzzling that scholastic theology might well be described as a kind of esoteric magic. The denser the darkness in which anyone shrouded a subject and the more he puzzled himself and others with preposterous riddles, the greater his fame for acumen and learning.

Nevertheless, his early training never deserted him. Always he was to think within the framework of the ideas of the schoolmen, and though it was to the fathers that he turned for an exposition of the faith, the Middle Ages are always present, only just hidden, in the *Institutes*. But, for the rest, when the time came, he was to educate himself in theology.

Obedient to his father's new intention, he left Paris and went to study law, first at Orleans for nearly a year, and then at Bourges. This was hard work, demanding the re-orientation of his mind, firmly settled in theology, to a new subject. And it was the harder for being uncongenial. But Calvin was a man of encyclopedic mind, born, like Dr. Johnson, to grapple with libraries.

Whatever subject he undertook to study, he mastered. And though it cost him his health, he mastered law so thoroughly that he was capable of deputizing for the professors when they wanted a day off. This labor was to have its reward when he came to the work of reshaping the Church in Geneva, and when for years he was to be embrangled in civic and national politics.

But during these years something more than a knowledge of the intricacies and niceties of the law was gained which he could never have won from the University of Paris. At Orleans and Bourges, the intellectual atmosphere was more free. New ideas were not bogies, but food for interesting speculation. The classics, those siren voices against which all good churchmen had closed their ears from the days of Gregory the Great, now seemed most desirable—calling, not to danger, but to delights.

Scholars snuffed and dug like terriers until they had laid bear the original sources, whether in the classics or the fathers or the Scriptures. Even Greek was taught, the key that unlocked the door to a new world. Calvin began to learn Greek. As to his Latin master, so to his Greek he later dedicated a Commentary—that on *II Corinthians*: "Nothing has had greater weight with me than the memory of when I was sent by my father to learn civil law. Under your direction and tuition I added to the study of law Greek literature, of which you were then a celebrated professor."

Certainly the few years in these two universities opened up a new world to a young man who had received such a conservative upbringing. The spirit of the Renaissance filled him, the spirit of free inquiry, of accurate scholarship and of good writing—the spirit of Greece and Rome. Not for his austere mind the lush and sensuous humanism of the South—"I only went to Italy," he used to say, "that I might have the pleasure of leaving it"—but of Erasmus with his passion for accurate editions, of Jacques Lefèvres, returning always to the original sources, of Reuchlin, the master of languages, of Montaigne who loved the manner of writing equally with the matter.

The few letters that remain from this time show his new outlook. They are more than a trifle precious, too carefully written—"an overdressed young man" as George Moore or somebody said of Stevenson. To his friend Francis Daniel of Orleans, this: "Your road-book I return, which, with Lampridius, we may call the itinerary, and in the Greek, *hodoiporikēn*. I do not add thanks, for words cannot do justice to its merits." More than a suspicion of *Love's Labor's Lost* there! But a few taffeta phrases may be forgiven in a man of twenty who has but lately breathed the fresh air of liberty and found it stronger than his sobriety.

For the present, dusty law was the serious work, literature only a delightful recreation. But after three years, his father died, and now he regarded himself as free to follow his own inclinations. He knew very well what he wanted to do. Five years earlier theology might have satisfied him. Now he could never be chained to the schoolmen like a book to its lectern. Law was even more distasteful. His recreation should be his work. He would be a humanist scholar after the pattern of the great Erasmus of Rotterdam.

Back, therefore, to Paris and the precarious life of the freelance writer and scholar. He still received the stipends of one or two livings to which, in the way of that lax age, he had been appointed as a boy to help with the expense of his education. But, even with this help, he frequently felt the pinch of scarcity of funds. At twenty-two, however, money is one of the less important worries in life. What mattered was that he was free to choose his own path, and that path wholly pleasant.

He set to work to write a commentary on a book of Seneca's called *De Clementia*. In 1532, it appeared, with a dedication to Claude de Hangest, his friend at Noyon and in Paris, and now an abbot in his hometown. Calvin, who had borne the cost of publication himself, was soon writing round to his friends asking them to use it in their lectures and to recommend it to likely purchasers. One copy he sent off to Erasmus.

His life seemed tolerably secure, his future, so far as he had the ordering of it, plain. Already at twenty-three he was a scholar of the first rank. He was happy in his circle of like-minded friends, and not unknown even at court. Yet eighteen months later he was escaping from Paris for his life. To see the reason for this, we must go backward in time and observe another force, and this decisive, working in his life.

At some time between 1528 and 1532, he had been converted to the teaching of the Reformation. When it happened we do not know. Calvin himself, in the autobiographical fragment prefacing the *Commentary on the Psalms*, merely tells us that it did happen. The date no longer interests him—"one thing I know, that whereas I was blind, now I see." Here is his account:

> When I was as yet a very small boy, my father destined me
> for the study of theology. But afterwards, when he consid-
> ered that the law commonly raised those who followed it
> to wealth, this prospect suddenly induced him to change
> his purpose. Thus it came to pass that I was withdrawn
> from the study of philosophy and set to the study of law.
> To this pursuit I endeavored faithfully to apply myself, in
> obedience to the will of my father. But God, by the secret
> guidance of His providence, at length gave a different di-

rection to my course. And first, since I was too obstinately devoted to the superstitions of popery to be easily extricated from so profound an abyss of mire, God by a sudden conversion subdued and brought my mind to a teachable frame, though I was more hardened in such matters than might have been expected from one at my early period of life. Having thus received some taste and knowledge of true godliness, I was immediately inflamed with so intense a desire to make progress therein, that although I did not altogether leave off other studies, I yet pursued them with less ardor.

Calvin was not a man to lay bare his soul. His innate reserve as well as his objective outlook kept him from it. He left behind him no spiritual autobiography, no *Confessions*, or *Grace Abounding for the Chief of Sinners*. He confesses that Jesus Christ is his Savior and his Lord, but he does not say how he arrived at that confession. Even Beza his friend and biographer, who as a boy lived in the same house with him in Bourges, can tell us nothing more.

But on just one occasion Calvin lifts the veil. He is writing to Cardinal Sadoleto, and puts into the mouth of an anonymous convert of Reformed preaching this confession. But though it is anonymous, he is almost certainly drawing upon his own story:

I, O Lord, always professed the same Christian faith in which I had been brought up as a boy. But at first I had no other reason for my faith than that which was then everywhere prevalent. Thy Word, which ought to have shone on all Thy people like a lamp, was taken away, or at least was hidden from us. And in case anyone should long for greater light an idea had been instilled in everyone's mind that the investigation of that hidden heavenly philosophy was better in the hands of a few whom the others might consult as oracles, and that the highest knowledge fit for plebeian minds was to subdue themselves to obedience to the Church. Again, the elements in which I had been instructed were such as could neither properly train me to the right and true worship of Thy divine majesty, nor pave the way for me to assure hope of salvation nor train me aright for the duties of the Christian life. I had indeed learned to worship Thee alone as my God; but since the true reason of worshipping was altogether unknown to me, I stumbled at the very threshold. I believed, as I had been taught, that I was redeemed by the death of Thy Son from condemnation to eternal death, but the redemption I envisaged was one whose efficacy could never reach to me. I looked for a future resurrection, but hated to think of it, as being an event most terrible. And this was not simply my own personal feeling, but was genuinely derived from the doctrine which was then uniformly preached to the people by their Christian teachers. They certainly preached of Thy mercy towards men, but confined it to those who could show that they deserved it. What is more, they placed this deserving in the righteousness of works, so that he alone was received into Thy favor who reconciled himself to Thee by works. Yet they did not disguise the fact that we are miserable sinners, that we often fall through the weakness of the flesh, and that to all, therefore, Thy mercy must be a haven of salvation. But the way to obtain it, according to them, was by making satisfaction to Thee for our offences. Then, again, the satisfaction they enjoined was, first, after confessing all our sins to a priest, humbly to ask for pardon and absolution; and secondly, to wipe out our bad actions from Thy remembrance by doing good deeds. Lastly, to supply what was still wanting, we were to add sacrifices and solemn expiations. Moreover, because Thou art a stern judge and a severe avenger of iniquity, they showed us how dreadful Thy presence must be. Therefore they bid us flee first of all to the saints, that by their intercession Thou mightest be won over and made friendly towards us.

But even when I had done all these things, though I had some periods of quiet, I was still a long way from true peace of conscience; for whenever I descended into my soul or raised my mind up to Thee, extreme terror seized me, such terror as no expiations or satisfaction could cure. And the more closely I examined myself, the sharper the stings with which my conscience was pricked, so that the only solace left to me was to delude myself by trying to forget it all. However, as nothing better offered, I continued on the path I had already begun.

But then a very different form of teaching arose; not one that led us away from the Christian profession, but one which brought us back to its fountainhead, and by, as it were, clearing away the dross, restored it to its original purity. Offended by the novelty, I lent an unwilling ear, and at first, I confess, strenuously and passionately resisted it; for—such is the firmness or willfulness with which men naturally persist in the course they have once undertaken—it was with the greatest difficulty that I was brought to confess that I had all my life been in error. One thing in particular made me averse to those new teachers; and that was reverence for the Church. . . . At last, my mind being prepared to give the matter serious attention, I saw—just as if light had broken in upon me—in what a pigsty of error I had wallowed, and how polluted and impure I had become. With great fear and trembling at the misery into which I had fallen, and far more at that which threatened me in the prospect of eternal death, I could do no other than at once betake myself to Thy way, condemning my past life, not without groans and tears.

Whenever this change took place, it was radical and decisive. By 1533, Calvin was whole-heartedly on the side of the Reformation. He was not yet a Reformer himself, was still apparently a member—at least outwardly—of the Roman Church, and wished still to pursue his life of scholarship without accepting, perhaps, the troubles that the Reformers had to bear.

"It was one thing," someone said of Philip Melanchthon, "to explain the Cross in theology, but another to suffer it in practice and experience." Calvin never relished the prospect of bearing the Cross, particularly in his earlier years. He had always, however much he might protest that he was ready to do his duty, to be forced into unpleasant decisions by circumstances. It was so now.

The Rector of the University of Paris, Nicholas Cop, was a close friend. On All Saints' Day, 1533—exactly sixteen years after Luther had nailed his Ninety-Five Theses to the Church Door at Wittenberg—Cop preached a university sermon in which he attacked the Paris theologians. The theologians, furious, retaliated and tried to have him arrested for heresy. He fled the country. Apparently Calvin had a hand in the composition of the sermon. He was also forced to flee, and escaped from Paris just in time to avoid arrest.

The story goes that he walked out of the city disguised as a workman. The storm very soon blew over, thanks chiefly to the intervention of the King's sister on Calvin's behalf. But his wanderings had begun. Paris, and indeed all France, held danger for him with the King in his present role as hammer of the heretics.

At length, after living with various friends, he arrived in Basel, and settled down once again to a life academic. In his two years of wandering, some time of which was spent in the house of Louis du Tillet with its splendid library, he had acquired a more extensive and precise knowledge of the fathers. Ambrose and Cyprian he now knew well, Chrysostom and Tertullian and above all the great Augustine, to whom he, like Luther, was drawn by strong bonds of theological sympathy.

Now in Basel he set to work in earnest on Hebrew. But always he complains of his own laziness. To Francis Daniel he writes: "considering the constitutional weakness and infirmity which you are well aware of, I am making some progress in study." And to Christopher Libertet of Neuchatel he remarks that, when he got to Basel, he sank down into his "wonted languor." He so far mastered his constitutional weakness, however, as to read many of the fathers, get a good working knowledge of Hebrew, and write another book. In the summer of 1535, he handed over to the printers the manuscript of the *Christianae religionis institutio*—or *The Principles of the Christian Religion*.

Calvin may now fairly be called an active Reformer. He is beginning to be known as a coming man. But he himself still conceives his activity as that of letters. Unencumbered by parochial or civic affairs, he would pursue the career of a writer—no longer a writer on the classics, but of theology.

His desires were those of the scholar—irresponsible in their simplicity and humbly arrogant—enough money to live without anxiety, a good library, and a peaceful life. "The summit of my wishes," he told Sadoleto, "was the enjoyment of literary ease, with something of a free and honorable station."

The portraits of Calvin we often see, though a few years later than this period, show us well enough the man and his character. The sharp-featured, keen, and intellectual face; the curly forked beard, well-tended; the large ring on the left hand, and the stylishly embroidered gloves he is holding; the sober but careful clothes with the pleated front and snowy ruff suggesting more than a little regard for his appearance—this is the portrait of the man who has enjoyed the society of the well-bred and the well-read. It is easy to understand this man desiring the "the enjoyment of literary ease with something of a free and honorable station."

But for some years Calvin had been learning the lesson which he found hardest for him—that his will was not the will of God, and that it is hard for man to oppose that will. Already in 1534 he had written to his confidant Francis Daniel: "I have learned from experience that we cannot see very far before us. When I promised myself an easy, tranquil life, what I least expected was at hand." This lesson had still to be learned thoroughly, and it was to take many years. Long after, he read his own experience into the character of the scribe who, in Matthew 8:19, offered to follow Jesus:

> We must bear in mind that he was a scribe, who had been accustomed to a quiet and easy life, had enjoyed honor and was ill-fitted to bear reproaches, poverty, persecutions, and the Cross. He wishes indeed to follow Christ, but dreams of an easy and agreeable life, and of dwellings filled with every convenience; whereas the disciples of Christ must walk among thorns, and march to the Cross amid uninterrupted afflictions. The more eager he is, the less he is prepared. He seems to want to fight in the shade and at ease, untroubled by sweat or dust, and beyond the reach of the weapons of war.

Very soon an occasion was to arise in which his obedience to the unexpected will of God was to be tested.

Returning from a visit to France, he was prevented by the uneasy state of the country, a war being in progress, from following the direct route, and made a detour which brought him through Geneva. His purpose was to spend the night in this city and then continue his journey towards Strassburg and literary ease.

But in Geneva was William Farel, the agent provocateur of the

French and Swiss Reformations. He learned of Calvin's presence, visited him, and asked him to help in the work of reforming the Genevan Church.

Calvin, when he had heard of the state of things in this turbulent city, refused. He was, he said, a scholar, not a man of affairs. Besides, he had no aptitude for such a work. He was shy and nervous, with none of Farel's force and courage. Tomorrow he was for Strassburg.

But Farel, this man who so often spoke unadvisedly with his lips, now spoke with prophetic power. "You are simply following your own wishes; and I declare in the Name of Almighty God that if you refuse to take part in the Lord's work in this Church, God will curse the quiet life that you want for your studies."

"I felt," says Calvin, "as if God from heaven had laid His mighty hand upon me to stop me in my course, . . . and I was so stricken with terror that I did not continue my journey."

# THE FIRST ATTEMPTS

The prospect of work in Geneva was uncongenial; release, when it came for a few years, most welcome; the return, torture. But until he should be set free by the hand of God Himself, Calvin regarded himself as bound to his position. He had not called himself to Geneva, and he could not dismiss himself. To the pastors of Zürich he wrote in 1541 when they were trying to persuade him to return to Geneva:

> Although it was a very troublesome province to me, the thought of deserting it never entered my mind. For I considered myself placed in that position by God, like a sentry at his post, from which it would be impiety on my part were I to move a single step. Yet I think you would hardly believe me were I to relate to you even a very small part of those annoyances, nay miseries, which we had to endure for a whole year. This I can truly testify, that not a day passed in which I did not long for death ten times over. But as for leaving that Church to remove elsewhere, such a thought never came into my mind.

We must pause here to look into what sort of a city this was that Calvin worked in. Its importance was far greater than its size. Although the population was quite small, its position on the borders of France, Switzerland, and Savoy gave it a strength without which it would not have been able to maintain its independence.

Before our story starts, Geneva had for a long time been subject simultaneously to three rulers—the Bishop of Geneva, the Counts of Savoy, and the four Syndics or Magistrates elected annually by the citizens. This unsatisfactory division of power led to friction and eventually war between the Bishop and Savoy on the one hand and on the other the citizens with their allies the cities of Berne and Freiburg. This was in 1530. When the citizens had won the war, the situation became rather easier for them. The Bishop remained Prince of Geneva, but the city now enjoyed self-government under three councils. This (apart from the Bishop, who disappears from the scene in 1536) was the constitution of Geneva as Calvin knew it.

The government of the city plays such an important part in Calvin's life that we must get its main outlines clear in our minds if we want to understand both the meaning of the struggle that went on for many years and also the significance of his work.

At the head was the Little Council, composed of the four Syndics, the treasurer and twenty others. It was elected by the Council of the Two Hundred, which, somewhat strangely, was in its turn elected by the Little Council. Between these two was the Council of the Sixty, each member of which sat also on the Council of the Two Hundred. Business went first to the Little Council, then to the Two Hundred. Any really serious decision could only be taken after it had been agreed upon by the General Council, which was composed of all the heads of households in the city. The four Syndics, who were elected by the General Council for at least two years at a time, were the leaders and presidents, and held greater power than would appear at first sight. If they had a majority in the Little Council, they could count also on a majority in the other two councils, and thus keep the rule in their own hands. During Calvin's life in Geneva we shall see this happening, with sometimes his friends and sometimes the disaffected in the seats of the mighty.

By the time Calvin arrived at the city, the Reformation was already an accomplished fact. The "new" opinions had infiltrated here in much the same way as elsewhere and brought in their train the usual opposition to the clergy (who are said, even by the opponents of the Reformation, to have been an unusually worthless lot) and many public disturbances. William Farel, who was working in western Switzerland in the early fifteen thirties, turned his attention to the place, at first in person, and when he was ejected, through his assistant, Antoine Froment. This Froment had a checked career and later was to become a great nuisance to Calvin; but at this time he was an ardent and useful Reformer. In Geneva he set up as a teacher of French, on the principle of money back if the pupil was not satisfied after a month. Whether he succeeded in teaching anyone to speak French in a month may be doubted; but he certainly won converts to the Reformed cause. They became sufficiently numerous to form a small Church and to worship and celebrate the Lord's Supper on their own. Soon Farel and Viret joined Froment, and under them the Reformed Church increased until it was permitted to hold occasional services in the churches. At last, in May 1535, after the General Council had forbidden the Roman priests to say Mass, Geneva became a Protestant city.

But there is a great difference between a legal constitution and a living Church. It was beyond the power of the city councils to make Geneva into an outpost of the kingdom of God. All they could do was to create a situation favorable to the preaching of the gospel and give their active support to that work.

After it had joined the Protestant ranks, Geneva was different from its earlier state only in that it contained a certain number of Reformed Christians and had a different Church. Its citizens remained as they had ever been; and it was here that the real issue lay as to whether the place was to be a Reformed city.

There was certainly plenty of room for reformation. Sixteenth-century manners were generally rough and sixteenth-century morals loose. But Geneva seems to have been rather worse than most towns. Riots had been frequent and bloody; some even of the ruling class had shown themselves Tybalts not unready with their swords. This was not to be suppressed in a day, and Calvin himself had to face some ugly situations. He was not unfamiliar with the sound of the mob outside his house threatening to throw him in the river and firing their muskets.

In regard to morals—that is to say, sexual morals—Geneva was distinguished by its licensed laxity. In every city in Europe men kept their mistresses; in Geneva a man was allowed to keep one mistress and no more. Every city had its brothels; in Geneva a special quarter was set apart for the prostitutes, who had their position further regularized by wearing distinctive dress and by being governed by one of their number as a sort of queen. It was this general situation that faced the Reformers, challenging them not only as honest citizens but above all as ministers of the Word of God.

Farel set manfully to work to translate the legal status into a spiritual reality. But building up was not a work for which he was fitted by nature. The *agent provocateur* is rarely also a statesman. When therefore in the midst of his troubles and perplexities Calvin appeared on the scene, Farel seized upon him thankfully and harnessed him to the work of reformation as his assistant. Before long the two were acting as equals and, along with the blind pastor, Elie Corauld, were the principal ministers in Geneva.

We can see from his writings Calvin's idea of the Church. There is no truth at all in the old statement that the Reformers were individualists, caring nothing for the Church. Because they broke with the Roman Church and gave up the Roman doctrine of the Church, it does not mean that they broke with any form of Church and held no doctrine of the Church. For Calvin the Church is "the mother of all who have God for their Father," and therefore,

> there is no other way of entrance into life but by our being conceived by her, nourished at her breast and continually preserved under her care and government until we put off this mortal flesh, and "become as the angels of God." For our infirmity will not permit of our leaving her school; we must continue under her instruction and discipline to the end of our lives. It must also be observed that out of her bosom there is no hope of remission of sins, or any salvation.

The Church is God's instrument for the salvation of His children; and the means He employs are the preaching of the gospel and the administration of the sacraments. Since this is so, these means of salvation are the marks by which we can discern the Church: "wherever we find the Word of God purely preached and heard, and the sacraments administered according to the institution of Christ, there, without any doubt, is a Church of God."

By the pure preaching of the Word of God, he meant the preaching of the biblical gospel in language familiar to the people. The proper administration of the sacraments entailed not only that the laity should communicate in both bread and wine, but also the exercise of discipline, by which flagrant offenders should be excluded from the Lord's Supper.

This was his conception of the Church, and this was what he strove to realize in Geneva. It was to be an established Church, comprising all the citizens of Geneva, and not simply a group of believers gathered from among them. But, on the other hand, he was not content to let it suffer the fate of so many national Churches, which became little more than the expression of the religious consciousness of the people. The Church must always be, if she is really to be the Church, a confessional Church. She must believe in Jesus Christ as Redeemer and Lord and must confess that faith openly in words and works. Calvin's aim in Geneva was to build up a Church that should be both national and confessional.

This aim he and his two colleagues pursued for the next two years—their chief endeavor to persuade the Councils to accept an ecclesiastical constitution that should spring from and embody Reformed doctrine. At the beginning of 1537, they were successful with a memorandum called *Articles on the Ruling of the Church.* It fell into four parts: on the Lord's Supper, hymn singing, the teaching of children, and marriage. It is the first that is the most important. It contains Calvin's basic idea of discipline, and it was to provoke the bitterest contention between the ministers and the Councils in Geneva. The Lord's Supper, said the *Articles,* ought to be celebrated every Sunday as in the early Church, but circumstances made it desirable for the present to celebrate only once a month. There must be a safeguard against unworthy participation, and the Church must have the right of excommunication. The most convenient method of putting the discipline into practice would be to have certain trustworthy men in the various quarters of the city to report on grave misdemeanors. The guilty should first be warned by the ministers, and then, if they proved obdurate, excommunicated until they repent.

Before long trouble began. Although the Councils had accepted the *Articles,* they refused to give effect to the recommendations on discipline. In this they undoubtedly had the larger part of public opinion on their side. The City Council of Berne interfered from political motives and fomented the dissension. Matters came to a head in 1538 when the Councils ordered that the Lord's Supper should be celebrated according to the use of the Church in Berne; and if the ministers refused to comply, they added, they would find others to take their place. Corauld was forbidden to preach, and imprisoned when he disobeyed. Calvin and Farel at first behaved with restraint, saying that they would accept the Berne use if it were ordered in a constitutional manner. This was unacceptable, for what the Councils were after was total surrender. They wanted to rule the Church as well as the city. The two Reformers were banned from the pulpit. The following day they both preached as usual. Thereupon all three were exiled from Geneva. After fruitless attempts to have the sentence withdrawn, they acquiesced and went their different ways—Farel to be minister at Neuchatel, Corauld into retirement, and Calvin first to Basel, where he hoped that he might once again pursue his quiet life of study.

There can be no doubt that some of the blame for the troubles in Geneva must be laid at the door of the Reformers. They did not sufficiently mingle tact with their firmness. Farel, indeed, was the least conciliatory of men, but Calvin also overstepped the bounds of propriety. It is one thing to feel strongly that your opponent is utterly wrong and a pernicious influence, but to call the city fathers of Geneva "a Council of the devil" in a sermon, as he did, might be thought more than a trifle provocative. In a letter to Farel six months alter, Calvin acknowledged their share in the way things had turned out:

> We may indeed acknowledge before God and His people, that it is in some measure owing to our unskillfulness, indolence, negligence, and error that the Church committed to our care has fallen into a sad state of collapse. But it is also our duty to assert our innocence and our purity against those who by their fraud, malignity, knavery, and wickedness have assuredly brought about this ruin. Willingly, therefore, do we acknowledge before God and all the godly, that our unskillfulness and carelessness deserved to be chastised by an example of this kind.

But he goes on to say that it would be false to accept the chief blame. Their motives were sound and their purpose good. It was in the execution of their purpose that they were at fault.

He was certainly in no way disposed to accept the interpretation that his friend and former host in that "quiet nest" at Angoulême, Louis du Tillet, put upon the affair. Has not all this trouble come upon you, he asked, as a correction from God to recall you to the true Church? Not so, replies Calvin. That his troubles were a chastening from God he freely agreed. But that his path was away from God and his Church was not true.

One of his companions in the conflict, Corauld, has already died and must now render an account before God. "When we come thither, it will be known on which side the rashness and desertion has been. It is thither that I appeal from the judgments of all the worldly-wise sages, who think their simple word has weight enough for our condemnation. There the angels of God will bear witness who are schismatics."

As for the future, his plans were uncertain. Du Tillet, in the same letter, offered to let him have as much money as he needed. Calvin declined, saying he had no need at the present. He had "seriously pondered the question of setting about gaining a livelihood in some private position." But while he was living in Basel, the "call motif," as we might term it, which runs through Calvin's life and had sounded so dramatically in Farel's arresting him for Geneva, again made its appearance.

The Church in Strassburg pressed him to take charge of the French congregation there. Calvin excused himself. Then Simon Grynaeus, with whom he was living at the time, the chief minister in Basel and a learned Grecian, told him he was enacting the part of Jonah, but the Lord would seek him out and find him as He did Jonah:

> Suppose to yourself that the Church should be lost through your fault alone. What better course of repentance lies open to you than to dedicate yourself wholly to the Lord? You who are endowed with such gifts, how can you, with a good conscience, decline this ministry that is offered to you?

He went to Strassburg, spending three moderately peaceful and happy years there, ministering to an appreciative Church of his fellow-countrymen, attending theological and ecclesiastical conferences, and doing some of his best writing.

# CHAPTER 3

# MAN OF LETTERS

Calvin was born to write.

Whatever course his life had taken, whether he had become a priest in the Roman Church or whether he had followed in the footsteps of Erasmus, he would still have been a writer. We might be tempted to say that, when Geneva claimed him, the Reformation was throwing away its greatest writer. And so, in one way, it was. He had inevitably less time to give to study and to the polishing of his sentences with the City Council worrying him about drains and heating apparatus, with ecclesiastical quarrels to settle with other Churches and worries and sickness in his own home.

But, in fact, he could hardly have written so voluminously if he had been allowed his quiet life in Strassburg or Basel. In the thirty-two years (almost to a day) between the publication of his first book and his death, he created by himself an entire and complete literature.

In the definitive edition of his works, the *Corpus Reformatorum*, his writings fill forty-eight quarto volumes printed in double column. There we find all his theological works, the *Institutes*, and many shorter pieces; the commentaries on the Scriptures and the eight-hundred-odd sermons; and ten and a half volumes of correspondence.

In his purely theological writing, the *Institutes* towers above the rest. Richard Hooker wrote,

> Two things of principal moment there are which have deservedly procured him honor throughout the world: the one his exceeding pains in composing the Institutions of Christian religion; the other his no less industrious travails for expositions of holy Scripture according unto the same Institutions. . . . Of what account the Master of Sentences was in the church of Rome, the same and more amongst the preachers of reformed Churches Calvin had purchased; so that the perfectest divines were judged they,

which were skillfullest in Calvin's writings. His books almost the very canon to judge both doctrine and discipline by.

The *Institutes* was not always the large volume divided into four books that we now know. Its beginnings were modest, and it arose in a way that we have grown unaccustomed to associate with dogmatic theology. We think of the dogmatic theologian writing almost in a vacuum; untroubled by events in the world, he evolves his abstract structure of ideas. Such a theologian would be of little use in the world. The *Institutes*, at any rate, sprang out of the contemporary situation in much the same way as, say, Heinrich Vogel's *The Iron Ration of a Christian* was written to meet the needs of members of the German Confessing Church under the Nazi regime.

During Calvin's years of wandering when he had fled from Paris and later while he was living in Basel, he had constant news of the trials of his countrymen. Their troubles culminated in the affair of the "Placards," when posters denouncing the Mass were displayed in prominent places in Paris. The anger of the King is understandable, his reaction, as a sixteenth-century monarch, inevitable. Within a month more than thirty Protestants were burned. A little after, however, international politics moved Francis to grant an amnesty. Calvin seized upon this favorable turn of events to address to him the small book of teaching he had written for laymen. He prefaced it with a letter to the King—"one of the great epistles of the world," it has been called.

> When I first set my hand to this task, most noble King, nothing was further from my mind than to write what is now presented to your Majesty. I intended only to put forward some elementary principles by which those who had been touched by some eagerness for religion might be fashioned to true piety. And this labor I undertook chiefly for our countrymen the French, of whom I saw many to be hungering and thirsting for Christ but very few who had any real knowledge of Him. That this was my design the book itself shows by its simple and straightforward form.
>
> But when I perceived that the fury of certain wicked men in your kingdom had reached such an extent

as to leave no room there for sound doctrine, I thought I should be well employed if in the same letter I were both to teach those whose religious education I had undertaken, and were to make my confession before you so that you might know the nature of that doctrine against which those furies rage with such madness who even now disturb your kingdom with sword and fire.

He concludes,

> But if your ears are so filled with the whispers of those who wish us ill as to leave no place for the accused to speak for themselves, and if those ruthless furies—with your connivance—continue to persecute so savagely with chains, scourgings, rackings, confiscation of goods, and the stake, we shall indeed, as sheep led to the slaughter, be reduced to the greatest extremities. Yet even so we shall in our patience still posses our souls, and we shall wait for the strong hand of the Lord, which in time will without doubt appear and show itself armed for the deliverance of the poor from their affliction and for vengeance upon those who despise them. May the Lord, the King of kings, establish your throne, most noble and illustrious King, with justice and your reign with equity.

If the book failed in its immediate purpose of influencing the King of France, it succeeded in another and ultimately more important direction. Here at least for the Reformed, as distinct from the Lutheran Church, was clear teaching on the faith delivered in the Scriptures. A Church cannot live without a theology, and a theology of the Scriptures at that. The Lutheran Church had already its dogmatics, for Philip Melanchthon had written his *Common Places* on the great Lutheran doctrines as early as 1521 and had been revising and enlarging it ever since. It is true that the Reformed Churches had Zwingli's *Commentary on True and False Religion* (besides an inferior little book by Farel, who was no theologian), but the way in which the *Institutes* so thoroughly supplanted the *Commentary* indicates that the earlier work was at least not sufficient for the needs of the Church.

When, at the age of twenty-six, Calvin wrote the *Institutes*, he gave the Reformed Church a firm and lasting theology.

The book was composed of only six chapters when it first appeared. The first three were expositions of the Ten Commandments, the Creed, and the Lord's Prayer; chapters four and five were on true and false sacraments; and the final chapter dealt with Christian liberty and ecclesiastical polity.

Before long, he was dissatisfied with it, and a more intimate knowledge of the fathers and the light thrown by practical work in Geneva and by theological conferences he attended led him to rewrite the book when he saw that it was well received. And indeed, for almost the whole of the rest of his life, he was at work on it, never satisfied until 1559—and even then, one wonders whether he would have been able to resist further revision if he had lived longer.

His first task was to translate the first edition from the Latin, the language of theologians, into French, so that it might be of use to the common man in his own country. Three years later, while he was exiled from Geneva in Strassburg, he republished the book in a larger form—nearly three times as long. This is in every way a handsome book; not only for the exceedingly pleasant proportions of the small folio and the fine printing, but also for the style of the writing.

Calvin was at his best as a writer during this Strassburg period. He was neither hindered by the press of business nor crushed under a burden of troubles as in his later life. In these three years, he gave us the 1539 Latin *Institutes* and the 1541 French translation of it, the *Epistle to Cardinal Sadoleto*, and the *Little Treatise on the Lord's Supper*. Each is a masterpiece. If he had died in 1541, he would still be recognized by succeeding ages as one of the greatest Reformed theologians and French stylists.

Every few years for the next twenty years, a new edition would appear, followed by its French counterpart. But until 1559, they were all variations and enlargements of the second edition. Then when he was seriously ill throughout the winter of 1558–1559, he had leisure to revise. He believed himself to be dying and spurred himself on to finish the final edition. He wrote in the preface,

> Last winter, when I thought that a quartan ague would
> quickly end in my death, the worse I became, the less I
> spared myself till I had finished this book, so that I might

leave it behind me as some grateful return to such kind solicitations of the religious public. I wish it could have been done sooner; but it is soon enough if well enough. I shall think it has appeared at the proper time when I find it has been more beneficial to the Church of God. This is my only wish.

Although large portions of the earlier editions were taken up into it, this was an entire remodeling. Instead of being divided simply into chapters, the last edition is in four books, each containing about twenty chapters. It is now arranged in conformity with the Apostles Creed:

Book I: The Knowledge of God the Creator
Book II: The Knowledge of God the Redeemer
Book III: How We Receive the Grace of Christ
Book IV: The Means of Grace

In this final form, it takes its place with the great theological writings of all ages—with Augustine's *City of God* and Peter Lombard's *Sentences*, with the *Summa Theologica* of Thomas Aquinas and the yet unfinished *Dogmatik* of Karl Barth.[1]

There seems little in common between the small book of six chapters and this *magnum opus*. A good many sentences survive all revising, but even so, usually in a new form. The teaching itself has not changed. What Calvin believed in 1536, he still believed in 1559—or, to shift the emphasis, what he believed in 1559 he already held in 1536. But, in fact, although he does not change, he continually develops. He sees that he has treated ideas true in themselves too briefly or without weighing the objections sufficiently, or that he could strengthen an argument with this or that patristic authority. In successive editions, we see him at work, building up the *Institutes* until he is at last satisfied that in subject and form he has given a "comprehensive summary and orderly arrangement of all the branches of religion."

When he had finished the final revision, all that remained was to translate it into French. This he did at once. Others soon put it into their own languages. In England, Thomas Norton (probably that same man

---

1 [When Parker wrote this in 1954, Barth was still working on his *Kirkliche Dogmatik* (Church Dogmatics) first published in 1932. Barth worked on his *Dogmatik* until his death in 1968.]

who wrote *Gorboduc*, one of the early Elizabethan plays) made a magnificent book out of it in 1561—

> So great a jewell was meet to be made most beneficiall, that is to say, applied to most common use. Therefore in the very beginning of the late Queenes most blessed raigne I translated it out of Latine into English, for the commodity of the Church of Christ. . . . I performed my worke in the house of my friend Edward Whitchurch, a man well knowne to be of upright heart and dealing, an ancient zealous Gospeller, as plaine and true a friend as ever I knew living, and as desirous to doe any thing to common good.

Edward Whitchurch's hospitality was well repaid; this translation is far better than the two nineteenth-century versions by Thomas Allen and Henry Beveridge. On the [European] Continent, it was translated in the sixteenth and seventeenth centuries into Dutch and Spanish, Italian, Bohemian, Hungarian, and German, perhaps even into Greek and Arabic. In the nineteenth century, the influence of what had been one of the widest read and most influential of all theological books waned until a German scholar could say in 1919: "Calvin's *Institutes* will probably be read even less in the twentieth century than in the nineteenth; and it will, as humanistic culture slowly decays, really become a foreign book to German and Swiss theologians." But in fact it has come into its own once again, and is being read more that at any time for the past hundred years.

* * *

Richard Hooker spoke of two things that "procured him on honor throughout the world": the *Institutes* and "his no less industrious travails for exposition of holy Scripture." And "industrious travails" it certainly was. Calvin wrote commentaries on every book of the New Testament, except Revelation. In the Old Testament, he wrote on the Pentateuch, Joshua, Psalms, and Isaiah. This is in addition to lectures he gave on the other prophets, which were afterwards published. He began his series of commentaries with *Romans* in 1540 and ended it with *Joshua* published after his death.

In those happy days, the writing of commentaries was not looked upon as the preserve of the linguistic, textual, or historical expert. Exact historical science as we know it today was then unknown, and the study of texts, a child of the Renaissance, was in its infancy. It was the theologian who wrote commentaries, and his purpose was to discover the theological meaning and significance of the original. Linguistics and textual reconstruction was a means to this end, not a goal in itself.

It was in this spirit and against this background that Calvin wrote his commentaries. He was a sound critic, well able to hold his own against the greatest of his day, even if he cannot be numbered among them. For example, in his *Commentary on Romans*, he is not afraid to dissent from Erasmus:

> Now as to the expression "the *impossibility* of the law" it is no doubt to be taken for defect or impotency—as though it had been said that a remedy had been found by God by which that which was an impossibility to the law is removed. The particle "in that" Erasmus has rendered "in that part in which," but as, I think it is to be causal I prefer to render it "because"; and though perhaps such a phrase does not occur among good Greek writers, yet as the apostles everywhere adopt Hebrew modes of expression, this interpretation should not be deemed improper. No doubt intelligent readers will allow that the cause of defect is what is here expressed, as we shall shortly prove again. Now, though Erasmus supplies the principal verb, yet the text seems to me to flow better without it. The copulative "and" has led Erasmus astray and made him insert the verb "has performed"; but I think it is used for the sake of emphasis.

At the bar of modern New Testament scholarship, Calvin would no doubt be judged wrong in using the word "because," but right in his main contention against Erasmus. The chief thing to notice is that his exposition of the New Testament rests upon a solid critical foundation. While he is not one of the really great textual critics—not an Erasmus or a Scaliger, a Bentley or a Housman—he is big enough to be independent in their company.

But his commentaries are not purely scientific investigations into ancient documents. He used what science his age afforded him to break through the artificial barriers separating him from the biblical writers so as to penetrate into their minds and, as it were, re-understand their ideas. Karl Barth says,

> How energetically Calvin, having first established what stands in the text, sets himself to re-think the whole material and to wrestle with it, till the walls which separate the sixteenth century from the first become transparent! Paul speaks, and the man of the sixteenth century hears.

* * *

Calvin's aim as a writer is to be understood, and he is able to match his purpose with his power, whether in Latin or in French. After the fall of the Roman Empire, Latin had changed its character, had become less literary and more homely, far closer to life and its realities. By classical standards, the most of medieval Latin is barbarous. Yet it has a pleasant homespun quality, even in the abstruse masters of theology. However that may be, the humanists of the fifteenth and sixteenth-century Renaissance despised it and set their wings for higher flights. "Choose for your reading," Erasmus advised the young Englishman Thomas Grey, "all the best authors . . . [and] read, among the first, Virgil, Lucian, Cicero, Lactantius, Jerome, Sallust and Livy."

But, above them all, it was Cicero who came into his own as the model for prose style. Conrad ab Ulmis, studying at Oxford in 1552, wrote home to his friend John Wolfius, describing his day's work: Aristotle from six to seven in the morning, then an hour on Roman law, at nine o'clock to the lecture of "that most eminent and learned divine, master doctor Peter Martyr," from ten to eleven on dialectics as propounded by Philip Melanchthon, and

> immediately after dinner I read Cicero's Offices, a truly golden book, from which I derive no less than a twofold enjoyment, both from the purity of the language and the

knowledge of philosophy. From one to three I exercise my pen, chiefly in writing letters, wherein, so far as possible, I imitate Cicero, who is considered to have abundantly supplied us with all instructions relating to purity of style.

From Mathurin Cordier in Paris, Calvin had caught the Ciceronian fever. From there on, all his writing is in the grand classical style. It is said, perhaps without truth, that throughout his life he read all Cicero yearly. His prose was the legacy of his early humanism.

Let a man once get a taste for good writing, and he will be fastidious to the end of his days. And Calvin had considerably more than a taste of letters when he was a young man. He took Pope's advice before it was given and drank deep of the Pierian spring. How deep, we can see from his one humanist book, the commentary on Seneca. Here he quotes from most of Cicero's works, from all Horace's, from Virgil and Ovid, from Terence, Homer, and Aristotle—in all, from fifty-six Latin writers and twenty-two Greek. When we reflect that he wrote the book before he was twenty-three, we can imagine the intense intellectual excitement in which he lived with the classics ever present in his mind. Like Mozart or Keats, or any other artist of genius, he is in these early years single-minded to the point of obsession.

When he underwent the radical upheaval and reversal of values that made him into a Reformer, theology elbowed the classics aside. His humanism is not in the foreground in his theological writings, though it remains an ever-present backcloth. In the *Institutes*, the Scriptures form a sort of pattern to his writing, not only when he is openly quoting a passage, but often the turn of a phrase will echo this or that in the Bible. And, besides the Bible, all his life he was reading and re-reading the fathers. Augustine was far and away his favorite, but he will turn also to Ambrose and Chrysostom, Jerome and Tertullian. His knowledge and application of the fathers expands perceptibly through the different editions of the *Institutes*, as even the acknowledged quotations show—though, in fact, he quotes very much oftener than the references say.

In the first edition, Augustine comes twenty times; three years later, one hundred and thirteen; then one hundred and twenty-eight in 1543, one hundred and forty-one in 1550, and finally no less than three hundred and forty-two in 1559. In the same way, Jerome advanced from three in the first edition to twenty-seven in the last. By contrast, it is interesting to notice that the mediaeval schoolman, Peter Lombard, who came next to Augustine in 1536 with thirteen quotations, only arrived at twenty-one by 1559.

These bare numbers give only a poor idea of how steeped Calvin was in early Christian literature. Others may have been more widely read than he. Hooker knew the Middle Ages better. Cranmer and Peter Martyr were perhaps his superiors on the fathers. John Jewel probably greater than them all on schoolmen and fathers. But nevertheless, Calvin's knowledge of the past was extensive. He knew most of the fathers intimately, and it is now realized that he knew the schoolmen far better than he used to be given credit for.

He did not live in the past, however, but kept abreast of the scholarship of his own time. Some part of Protestant theology was closed to him since he had neither German nor English. This gap in his equipment was less serious then than it would be now, since a knowledge of Latin took one most of the way. It was mostly popular works that were written in the common tongue. Technical theology was in Latin, and in that language it is plain that he read widely in his contemporaries, not only among the Protestants, but also of other schools—for example, there still exists a copy of one of Sir Thomas More's books with Calvin's name in it and the date in which he bought it (which, incidentally, was the same year it appeared).

Calvin's Latin style was noble, but his French was creative. It is interesting that the Reformation helped to form the languages of Europe. In England, the Prayer Book and the Authorized Version of the Bible; in Germany, Luther's writings and especially his translation of the Bible; in Denmark, Christiern Pedersen, "the first Danish writer of importance."

But in French, Calvin must share the honor of being the "father of French prose" with a very different writer, Rabelais (whom he liked not at all). It is chiefly upon the 1541 translation of the *Institutes* that the title rests: "this translation is one of the *chefs-d'oeuvre* [literary masterpiece] of the sixteenth century. It created an epoch," says a French literary historian.

His prose style is characterized by its clarity and precision, dignity and brevity. He always knows just what he wants to say, and always knows just how to say it. He is usually brief and has no place for ornament as such—"he despised mere eloquence," said Theodore Beza, "and was sparing in the use of words." His is indeed a prose style. We must not look for poetry in Calvin, for a poet he most certainly was not. He wrote one Latin poem, but could have employed his time more usefully. Nor had he any fundamental sympathy with poetry. He had read a good deal, no doubt, but it would be hard to imagine him rolling Virgil round his tongue or delighting in his own countryman, Pierre Ronsard. His prose is not poetic. But it is going too far to say with Earnest Dowden that it lacks grace. Take this, for example, from the *Excuse to the Nicodemites*, even in an inadequate translation:

> Without flattering them in their sin, I have exhorted them to pray continually to God, confessing their poverty with sorrow and trembling, that they may obtain pardon: I have exhorted them to commend themselves to Him, praying Him that, by His infinite goodness, it may please Him to deliver them from their captivity, or else to give them strength and constancy to prefer the honor of His Name to their own life.

What his prose does lack, however, is poetic imagination. The gravity of this fault depends on our view of the nature and purpose of prose. If we regard the Jacobean splendor of Richard Hooker or the baroque magnificence of Jeremy Taylor as the norm of prose, then no doubt Calvin's prose seems unexciting. If on the other hand, we are concerned with how to communicate ideas, we shall time and time again be struck dumb with admiration at his transparent ease when dealing with even the most abstruse problems. His artistry is of the highest order; it has to be sought for.

A fine scholar, a powerful intellect, a great creative artist—Calvin was all these. But we should have poorly understood him as a man of letters if that were all we had to say of him. He himself speaks very differently. Without doubt, all pride apart, he knew his own intellectual stature. Part at least of his certainty was the sublime arrogance of the artist, the arrogance of

> *So long as men can breathe, or eyes can see,*
> *So long lives this, and this gives life to thee.*

But he knew also that there was another word to be said. He wrote because it was natural to him to write, but he harnessed this faculty to the service of God, and his writing was all of a piece with the rest of his life, a living sacrifice to the service of God in the Church and in the world. It is striking that when he became a Reformer, he had done with secular writing. Henceforward, he became, as a man of letters, the minister of the Word of God.

When I was an undergraduate, one of our lecturers presented us with a booklist containing over ninety titles. Daunted, I read none of them. One might feel the same before the fifty volumes of the Calvin Translation Society. How should one set about reading Calvin? Most people start with the *Institutes* and make rather heavy weather of Book I. The *Institutes* needs working up to and should only be attempted when one has a taste for Calvin and some knowledge of others of his works.

I would suggest that the *Commentary on St. John's Gospel* makes a good introduction to Calvin, and after that one might go on to the *Commentary on Ephesians*. At the same time, one might dip into his letters. If, after this, one's blood is up and the hunt for what Calvin can give us is on, we can go straight for the *Institutes*, either reading it right through, or, better still, picking out subjects that have a particular interest for us and reading those chapters to see what Calvin has to say about them. After that, we have the whole of the fifty volumes to browse in as we will.

A word on editions. In the original languages there are three: Geneva, 1617, in seven folio volumes; Amsterdam, 1671, in nine folio volumes; and the biggest and completest edition in the series called *Corpus Reformatorum*, in which it occupies volumes 29–87. The best Latin edition of the *Institutes* is in volumes 3–5 of the *Calvini Opera Selecta*, edited by Peter Barth and Wilhelm Niesel. In English, the usual edition of the works is the Calvin Translation Society, published at Edinburgh in the nineteenth century, and now being reprinted in America. It contains commentaries, theological tracts, and the *Institutes*, but no sermons. This edition is not at all well edited, and there are sometimes faults in the translation. For those who prefer the excitement of Elizabethan prose to the stiff writing of the mid-nineteenth century, many of his works are available in early translations, including some volumes of sermons that have not been translated since.

The *Institutes* can be read in three translations. It was first put into English by Thomas Norton in 1561. This, from the point of view of style, easily holds the field. A Truro schoolmaster, Thomas Allen, translated it again in 1813—a fair translation, though not exciting to read and not so literal as a scientific book should be. Finally came Henry Beveridge for the Calvin Translation Society. This is the translation most frequently used. I myself find it dull, and my loyalty is given to Thomas Norton. Those who have Latin or French will find great pleasure in the 1539 Latin and the 1541 French editions. To work with original copies of either the 1539 or the 1559 *Institutes* is an added pleasure. A young student of Calvin will not soon forget the thrill he used to experience when he worked with a copy of the final edition—a really magnificent folio—which Calvin himself had given to an English bishop.

CHAPTER 4

# THE THEOLOGIAN

It was a pleasant habit of the Middle Ages to give their theologians a title of honor which at the same time emphasized their chief characteristic. Duns Scotus, with his quiddities, they called the Subtle Doctor. Bonaventura, scaling the Heavenly ladder, became the Seraphic Doctor. Thomas Aquinas, "above the rest in shape and gesture proudly eminent," was named the Angelic Doctor. Fortunately, we have no need to invent such a name for Calvin, since Philip Melanchthon has already done it for us.

At the Conference at Worms in 1541, overwhelmed by Calvin's learning and theological acumen, he called him The Theologian. No more needed to be said. Just as to the Middle Ages Aristotle had been *The Philosopher* and St. Paul *The Apostle*—so that if you had mentioned *The Philosopher*, everyone would have known you meant Aristotle—so Calvin is to Melanchthon, *The Theologian*. And, indeed, it would be hard to find his equal as a dogmatic theologian. Augustine and Luther were perhaps his superiors in creative thinking; Aquinas in philosophy; but in systematic theology Calvin stands supreme.

We have already seen in the third chapter that Calvin was not an ornamental writer. He rarely uses imagery. But that makes the few images he does use all the more lively and significant. There are certain images that constantly recur throughout his writings, and they show us clearly the way his mind was working. One that we are always meeting is the Labyrinth. Another is the Schoolmaster. If we examine them now they will throw a great deal of light on his theology.

It does not much matter what labyrinth Calvin had in mind— probably the Greek legend of Theseus, who penetrated the labyrinth at Cnossus, slew the Minotaur, and found his way out again by means of the thread which Ariadne had given him. But whether it was that, or whether it was the labyrinth in Egypt, one of the seven wonders of the world, or whether he was thinking of some other maze, his meaning is perfectly clear. Man is lost in a maze, of which he does not possess the plan, and however much he may attempt to find his way out, he always fails. He can never know God by himself, for his sin has led him into ignorance and a wrong-mindedness that prevents him from thinking his way through to the true idea of God. His mind is a veritable maze, with passages leading off to the worship of this or that idol. He has to worship some god, and he will invent a god, or perhaps many gods, to worship:

> Men's conceptions of God are formed, not according to the representations He gives of Himself, but by the inventions of their own presumptuous imaginations. . . . They worship, not God, but a figment of their own brains in His stead.

For all his capabilities, man is a puzzled, groping creature, surrounded by that which is mysterious to him. He not only does not understand God, nor does he understand the world in which he lives, but he does not even understand himself—from where he has come, why he lives, or to where he goes. If help does not come to him from without, he will never know God or find His kingdom.

But God, in His loving concern for man, reaches right to him, where he is wandering imprisoned in the labyrinth, and gives him the guidance of the Holy Scriptures, which are like a thread, leading him through this maze of ignorance to the knowledge of God. "The light of the Divine countenance, which the Apostle himself says 'no man can approach unto,' is like an inexplicable labyrinth to us, unless we are directed by the thread of the Word."

The basis of Calvin's theology, therefore, is the belief that through the Bible alone can God be known in His wholeness as the Creator, Redeemer, and Lord of the world. He is not so discernible in any other place—in the creation, or in man's conscience, or in the course of history and experience. And since, if we are to know of God, we must go to the place where He is to be found, it is to the Scriptures that we must go, and there we shall find Him as He is. If a man asks us to meet him in Piccadilly Circus, it is there (if he will and can keep his word) that we shall find him, and not in Trafalgar Square. The Scriptures are not man's guesses about the mystery of God, nor are they the conclusions that men have drawn from certain data at their disposal. On the contrary, they are the unveiling of the mystery of God by God Himself—God's gracious revelation of Himself to ignorant and sinful men. Far from being a stage, even the last stage, on man's quest for the well at the world's end, the Bible is the place where God comes from above and beyond the world to show Himself to

His people.

There is nothing Calvin dislikes more than speculation. Speculation is man's bypassing the Scriptures so as to arrive at some idea of his own about God, and it is also a going beyond Scripture, so as to enquire into mysteries on which the Bible is silent. How often in his sermons he exhorts the congregation to beware of man's own ideas, and to hold fast to the Scriptures! "When we enter into the pulpit it is not so that we may introduce our own ideas and dreams." And in the *Institutes*, we find a sustained attack against speculation, in whatever guise it may show itself.

> The very unhappy results of this temerity should warn us to study this question with more docility than subtlety, and not allow ourselves to investigate God anywhere but in His sacred Word, or to form any ideas of Him but such as are agreeable to His Word, or to speak anything concerning Him but what is derived from the same Word.

This is Calvin's theological program—to build on the Scriptures alone.

This brings us to the second image, that of *the Schoolmaster*. He pictures the relationship between God and man as that of master and pupil. God is the Schoolmaster. The school or lessons are the Scriptures. Man is the pupil. Once again it must be remembered that in ourselves we are ignorant of even the elements of the knowledge of God: "This, then, must be considered a fixed principle, that, to enjoy the light of true religion, we ought to begin by being taught from heaven; and that no man can have the least knowledge of true and sound doctrine, without having been a pupil of the Scriptures." The only place where we can learn is the Scriptures, since they are the teaching which God Himself gives us.

God is the Schoolmaster in two senses, though in the end these fuse into one single idea. First of all, the writings of the Bible owe their origin to God. Certainly, the Bible was written by men—Isaiah, Malachi, John, Paul, and the rest. And what is more, they were capable of making mistakes. Calvin was certainly no fundamentalist. When he came across a mistake, he acknowledged it without more ado, and it seems not to have worried him. For example, when he is commenting on Matthew 27:9 ("Then was fulfilled that which was spoken by Jeremy the prophet"), he says: "I confess I do not know how the Jeremiah came in here, and I do not worry much.

Certainly it is an obvious mistake to put Jeremiah for Zachariah, for we do not find this saying or anything like it in Jeremiah."[1] Yet nevertheless, despite their human and fallible writers, the Scriptures ultimately come to us from God Himself. God has spoken, and, inspired by Him, men have passed on His Word in writing. For all its human quality, the Bible is not only the "word" of its human writers but the Word of its Divine inspirer. So, in the Scriptures, God teaches us about Himself, about ourselves and about the world we live in. In this way He is our Schoolmaster.

But, plain as the Scriptures are, the blindness of our understanding is such that they are above our comprehension. If we were left to ourselves in trying to understand and profit from this book, we should fail totally. We should be like a child who can read only English being set to work on a Latin book. We speak only the language of mankind; the Bible speaks the language of God. "For my thoughts are not your thoughts, neither are your ways my ways, saith the Lord. For as the heavens are higher than the earth, so are my ways higher than your ways, and my thoughts than your thoughts" (Isa. 55:8–9). We need an interpreter if we are to understand the thoughts and ways of God as they are set before us in the Bible. And, as the hymn says,

> *God is His own interpreter,*
> *And He will make it plain.*

Not only do the Scriptures come from God in the first place, but also He enlightens our minds that we may understand what they mean. God is therefore the Schoolmaster in this second sense. The Holy Spirit Himself teaches us what the Bible means; and He teaches us, moreover, not in the way of a scientific lesson only, but drives it home both to our minds and also to our wills, so that we may not only understand with our minds, but also believe with our hearts, and be converted.

Those who submit themselves to this teaching will not only receive certain ideas about God, but they will be transformed by the knowledge of Him into His image. You can tell a man's school by his character, says Calvin, and the man who has been to school in the Scriptures will always bear the mark of it. "If a scholar is a man of parts," he says in a sermon on 2 Timothy, "and his master is a good teacher too, he will certainly not <u>only remember </u>what he has been taught, but will also retain some

1 [Calvin also has been understood as meaning that the errors came in through subsequent copyings of the text.]

characteristic of his master, so that it will be said, 'He was at such and such a school.'"

Now, since that is so, it is to the school of the Scriptures that we should go if we wish to learn to know God. But it is one of the faults of our sinfulness—according to Calvin, it is the very heart of our sinfulness—that we imagine we need no help to know God. We are high-minded as the Psalmist would say. Therefore, the first step we have to take is to become as little children, who are ignorant of the very first principles. We have to acknowledge our ignorance and submit to being taught. This humble submission or obedience to the voice of the Holy Spirit in the Word of God is a mark of the believer, for "my sheep hear my voice."

It is clear that Calvin's intention was to build his theology on the teaching of the Scriptures alone, to be guided in all his thinking by the Bible, and to refuse all other guides and masters. This means, of course, that the only judgment that he would recognize as valid is the judgment of the Scriptures. We miss the mark if we judge his theology by any other standard. It stands or falls according to its faithfulness to the Word of God. Let us now see whether in the chief respects Calvin is successful in carrying out his aim. We must confine ourselves to the chief points, for plainly a detailed study of the Scripturalness of his theology would take a very long essay.

Without doubt the chief concern of the New Testament—and in the last resort its only concern—is with Jesus Christ. The four Gospels are occupied entirely with Him; the other figures who come into the story are present not because they have an independent importance of their own, but solely because of their relationship to Him and His story. The Acts of the Apostles, although it tells us about the life of the apostolic Church, makes it plain that the importance of the apostles lies in their being the bearers of the gospel about Jesus Christ. Luke is not really interested in church history as such, nor in apostolic biography. What he wishes to show is how the apostles and others preached about Jesus Christ, and how the life of the Church was built upon Him. In Acts, Luke writes of what Jesus Christ went on doing in His Church after He had ascended. The writers of the epistles have the same theme of Jesus Christ, whether it is Paul summarizing his gospel as "I determined not to know anything among you, save Jesus Christ, and him crucified," or whether it is Hebrews exhorting us to "consider him," or Peter seeing Him as the "chief cornerstone, elect, precious," or John declaring "the Word of life" which he had seen and touched. They are all writing primarily about Jesus Christ. The chief concern of the New Testament is with Him. He occupies the central place in the faith and witness of the early Church.

Now this centrality of Christ is also the first fact to be noticed in Calvin's theology, in its scientific form in the *Institutes* and in its pastoral form in the Sermons. In a passage in his *Commentary on Colossians*, he says what may well be taken as his theological program:

> Again Paul returns to thanksgiving, that he may take this opportunity of enumerating the blessings which had been conferred upon them through Christ; and thus he enters upon a full delineation of Christ. For this was the only remedy for fortifying the Colossians against all the snares by which the false apostles endeavored to entrap them— to understand accurately what Christ was. For how comes it that we are "carried about with so many strange doctrines" (Hebrews 13:9), but because the excellence of Christ is not perceived by us? For Christ alone makes all other things suddenly vanish. Hence there is nothing that Satan so much tries to effect as to call up mists so as to obscure Christ; because he knows that by this means the way is opened up for every kind of falsehood. *This, therefore, is the only means of retaining, as well as restoring, pure doctrine: to place Christ before the view such as He is with all His blessings, that His excellence may be truly perceived.*

This is the place he set out to give to Christ in his theology. But we must say right at the outset that unfortunately he was not always consistent. On one major point, he was not so clear as he ought to have been, and on another he did not always keep in mind his principle of "Christ alone." In both he failed to give to Christ the centrality that is such a magnificent feature of most of his theology.

The first point concerns the knowledge of God the Creator, which is the subject of the first book of the *Institutes*. The problem of natural theology, of a knowledge of God gained apart from Christ, was not the burning question in the sixteenth century that it has become today. What was at issue then was rather the uniqueness of Christ in justifying and sanctifying the sinner. And on this issue, there cannot be the slightest doubt where Calvin stands. But, unfortunately, there is doubt on his attitude to natural theology, since he seems to make certain concessions, very guardedly, to man apart from the redemption in Christ.

This is a thorny and highly technical subject, and there is no need to go into it now. Sufficient to mention that two books on it appeared almost together at the beginning of 1952, and, with the same facts to work on, came to somewhat different conclusions. The very fact that this could happen shows that Calvin spoke considerably less clearly than he does usually, and that he did not give, without ambiguity, the central place in the knowledge of God the Creator to Jesus Christ.

The second point brings us to predestination—bad-temper and predestination, the two things that make Calvin particularly terrible! The trouble here is that he seems to have taken over the classical church doctrine of predestination (perhaps because he saw in it an excellent witness to the primacy and initiative of God in salvation) and tried to fit it into the framework of salvation in Jesus Christ. It was not, of course, a doctrine that he made up; it had already had a long history in the Church. Augustine had given it its distinctive shape. Thomas Aquinas taught it as boldly and clearly as Calvin.

Let us briefly see what Calvin teaches and say where we think he was at fault. God, before He made man, says Calvin, decreed the eternal future of every single human being. Some He chose to be His children. Others he destined to damnation.

> Predestination we call the eternal decree of God, by which He has determined in Himself what He would have to become of every individual of mankind. For they are not all created with a similar destiny; but eternal life is foreordained for some, and eternal damnation for others. Every man, therefore, being created for one or the other of these ends, we say, he is predestined either to life or to death.

This, says Calvin, as he contemplates with horror the abyss of eternal damnation, is a terrifying thought.

What is wrong here? It is that in all this definition there is no mention at all of Christ. Of course, Calvin saw the need of linking up the idea of predestination with Christ, and as far as the election to eternal life goes, he will always say, with Ephesians, that we are chosen "in Christ." But he does not always work this out consistently. We are left, as it were, with a God who is in two minds about mankind. One purpose of God is in Jesus Christ, and another purpose of God seems to have nothing to do with Christ. We get the impression that Calvin is trying to work the doctrine into his theology, instead of working it out from the center—Christ. His doctrine of predestination, like his doctrine of the knowledge of God the Creator, needs correcting to make it consistent with Calvin himself.

Leaving these two blemishes behind us (and we may note in passing that though each calls for a major operation, it does not demand a removal of the heart of his theology), we can go on with our comparison between the Christology of the New Testament and of Calvin. We have already said that, like the New Testament, he gives the central place to Christ. But what is this place in the Bible? By turning to a few of those places where the writers summarized their gospel, we shall arrive at the answer to this question. Such passages are Acts 2:14ff. and 3:12–26; 1 Corinthians 15:1ff.; and Romans 1:1–4.

Peter's sermon on the day of Pentecost may be summed up like this: The astounding fact of the apostles speaking in other tongues is to be ascribed to the Holy Spirit who, according to the prophecy in Joel, has now been given. But the Holy Spirit has been given because of Jesus of Nazareth, the man whom they have crucified, but whose crucifixion was the purpose of God, and who has been raised from the dead and made Lord and Christ.

His sermon a little later in the Temple (Acts 3:12–26) is very similar. The people had denied Jesus and caused Him to be killed. But His death is the fulfillment of the purpose of God, who has raised Him from the dead and will send Him at "the time of the restitution of all things."

In 1 Corinthians 15:1–4, Paul reminded the Corinthian Church what it was that he had preached to them in the beginning: "how that Christ died for our sins according to the Scriptures: and that he was buried, and that he rose again the third day according to the Scriptures."

And in his prologue to Romans (1:1–4), he says that he was set apart to preach the gospel, which had been promised in the Old Testament, and which was "concerning his Son Jesus Christ our Lord which was made of the seed of David according to the flesh, and declared to be the Son of God with power, according to the spirit of holiness, by the resurrection from the dead."

All these passages have as their core the death and resurrection of Jesus Christ. They also say that this was what had been promised as the purpose of God by the Old Testament. Moreover, Jesus, who as man is of the house of David and yet is also the Son of God, is the Lord and the Messiah, and He will come again to restore the creation. The apostolic gospel, therefore, is that the Son of God became man in the line of the Jewish king David; He was killed by the malice of His enemies, and yet according to His purpose God raised Him from the dead and exalted Him to authority and power as Lord of Heaven and earth; finally, He will return in judgment, and to restore all things.

What we have now to ask is whether Calvin catches the note of this gospel and faithfully passes it on in his theology. Calvin emphasizes in Christ especially His glory and humility and relates them both to the human situation of need and wretchedness. Jesus of Nazareth is the Son of God, in all eternity one with the Father in His glory. "Before the creation of the world," he says in his *Commentary on Philippians* 2:6, "Christ was in the form of God, because from the beginning He had His glory with the Father. . . . For in the wisdom of God, before He assumed our flesh, there was nothing mean or contemptible, but, on the contrary, a magnificence worthy of God."

When He became man, it meant that He humbled Himself, and humbled Himself still further to become such a man as He was—a man of sorrows, outcast, suffering, dying in dereliction on the Cross. And yet He had not ceased to be the Son of God. His glory was not diminished but hidden "under the veil of His flesh"—that is, it was hidden by His being a man, and such a man as He was. The glory of the Son of God was hidden in Jesus, save when He willed to display it, as He did in His teaching and His miracles, so that those to whom He thus revealed Himself (as for example, Peter at Caesarea Philippi or the disciples on the mount of transfiguration) recognized and confessed Him as the Christ, the Son of God.

Yet the course of the life of Jesus was characterized by suffering and humiliation from beginning to end, the suffering becoming more intense and the humiliation ever deeper until the final cataclysm of the Cross. But the suffering was not accidental. It represented, on the one hand, the purpose of God and, on the other, the total obedience of Jesus to that purpose. By His being obedient to the extent of dying the death that He died, He was the sacrifice for the sin of the world. Our sin against God is transferred to this willing sacrifice who makes atonement for us by His death, so that we are forgiven by God, who also accepts us as His own children. In an interesting passage in the *Institutes*, Calvin summarized the gospel that he himself preached. When we preach, we must tell a man

> that he was alienated from God by sin, an heir of wrath, liable to the punishment of eternal death, excluded from all hope of salvation, a total stranger to the blessing of God, a slave to Satan, a captive under the yoke of sin, and, in a word, condemned to and already involved in, a horrible destruction; that, in this situation, Christ interposed as an intercessor; that He has taken upon Himself and suffered the punishment which by the righteous judgment of God impended over all sinners; that by His blood He has expiated those crimes which make them odious to God; that by this expiation God the Father has been duly satisfied and atoned; that by this intercessor His wrath has been appeased; that this is the foundation of peace between God and men; and that this is the bone of His benevolence towards them.

The last word is not with the death of the Cross, however, which in itself is incomplete without the Resurrection. In the Cross and Resurrection, we see the humility and the glory of Christ in their most intense and profound forms. Jesus has conquered sin, death, and the devil. Now the Resurrection is the sign of His victory as well as being a part of it. From here on, He is the Lord over all, with authority in heaven and on earth, the Shepherd of His Church.

> He sits on high that from thence He may shed forth His power upon us, that He may animate us with spiritual life, that He may sanctify us by His Spirit, that He may adorn His Church with a variety of graces, and defend it by His protection from every calamity, that by the strength of His hand, He may restrain the fierce enemies of His Cross and of our salvation; finally, that He may retain all power in heaven and on earth, till He shall have overthrown all His enemies, who are ours also, and shall have completed the building up of His Church. And this is the true state

of His kingdom, this the power which the Father has con-
ferred upon Him, till He completes the last act by coming
to judge the living and the dead.

Calvin's gospel, like that of the Scriptures, is concerned with Jesus Christ.
It is concerned with Him as the Son of God and the suffering Servant; as
the one who has died for our sins and risen again for our justification; as
the eternal Lord. He emphasizes the place he gives to Christ and makes it
explicit by working it out in regard to the whole of theology (with, as we
have seen, some inconsistencies) and of the life of the Church and of the
individual Christian. This is the meaning of those famous battle cries of
the Reformation: *Sola gratia! Sola fide!—By grace alone! By faith alone!* We are
saved by the grace of God alone, and not by anything that we could con-
tribute; but the grace of God is His love towards us in Jesus Christ.

> Not only, therefore, does He declare that the love of God
> is free, but likewise that God displayed it in the riches, the
> extraordinary and preeminent riches of His grace. It de-
> serves notice also that the name of Christ is repeated; for
> no grace, no love, is to be expected by us from God except
> through His mediation.

And if our salvation is by grace alone, it follows that it is by faith alone,
for to rely on grace only is to give up any trust in our own capabilities or
capacity for salvation.

When we have nothing, but turn to God in Christ to supply our
need, we are believing. For faith is the acknowledgement of our own pov-
erty and the prayer for God's riches in Christ.

To deny *sola gratia* and *sola fide* is to deny the uniqueness and wor-
thiness of Christ as our Savior. If we would understand Calvin's theology—and, indeed, his whole life work—we must approach it from what he
says about Jesus Christ and take in all seriousness the purpose that he de-
clares in his *Commentary on Colossians* 1:12: "This therefore is the only means
of retaining as well as restoring pure doctrine—to place Christ before the
view just as He is, with all His blessings, that His excellence may be truly
perceived."

# CHAPTER 5

# NUMBER ELEVEN
# RUE DUE CHANOINES

All this while, Geneva was not forgotten.

Calvin and Farel were kept informed of affairs in the city by their friends yet remaining there. They were told that things were going from bad to worse. Their discipline was overthrown, and with it fell the moral improvement for which they had striven. The ministers appointed in their place were neither numerous nor strong enough to oppose the Council.

With the Church reduced to such straits, the Romanists made an attempt to win Geneva back. Cardinal Sadoleto, a man who stood for moderate reform within the Roman Church, wrote to the citizens, exhorting them to return to the fold. His hope failed: Geneva had not thrown off the Reformed yoke merely to submit again to the Roman. It was some comfort to the Reformers that this peril had been averted. But things were too bad in other directions for them to be happy. Their opponents had, in fact, won a complete victory.

But the victory was too complete. The leaders of the opposition were overtaken by the whirlwind they had created. First, one of the Syndics was sentenced to death for killing a man in a riot. Then, two others were convicted of treason and fled the city. Yet another broke his neck jumping from a window to escape arrest on a charge of sedition. The voice of scandal was raised, with good reason, against the ministers themselves. The moral state of the city became more and more alarming. It began to look, too, as if Berne, whose advice had been so eagerly sought previously, was now advising rather more frequently than the independence of Geneva approved. At last things came to such a pass that the city began to look back with some nostalgia to the more sober and orderly days of Calvin. As Richard Hooker put it unforgettably, "they were not before so willing to be rid of their learned pastor, as now importunate to obtain him again from them who had given him entertainment."

The learned pastor, however, when he received the call to return, was filled with alarm and wished himself anywhere but in Geneva. His first reaction came in a letter to Farel: "I would submit to death a hundred times rather than to that cross on which I had daily to suffer a thousand deaths." "The more that time passes," he writes a month later, "the more clearly do I see what a whirlpool of danger the Lord has delivered me from." And he was determined not to go back. His friends began to press him. Viret naïvely suggested that Geneva was good for his health. He replied grimly: "I could not read that passage in your letter without a smile where you show so much concern for my health and recommend Geneva on that score. Why could you not have said at the cross? It would be far better to perish once for all than to be tormented again in that torture chamber. Therefore, my dear Viret, if you wish me well, do not mention such a proposal."

Nevertheless, such was the chorus of admonition from his friends, "throwing me for two days into such perplexity and trouble of mind that I was scarcely myself," that he was forced to consider the matter seriously, even if only that he might give a reasoned refusal.

Once he was in Geneva he had no right to leave, he told Farel, but that was not the same as going back when he had been expelled. Besides, what use would he be, one man perhaps alone against many? In Strassburg, he is happy and useful. Why should he go where he may be less useful and certainly unhappy? Yet in the last resort, he would not commit himself to a straightforward refusal. He had often enough called Geneva a cross, and he could not escape the word of Christ that His disciples must bear the Cross if they would follow Him. Calvin, therefore, began to hesitate: "It is my desire that the Church of Geneva shall not be left destitute. Therefore, I would rather venture my life a hundred times over than betray her by my desertion. But since my mind does not move me spontaneously to return, I am ready to follow those who, there is some good hope, will prove safe and trusty guides to me."

Once he had come to this frame of mind, his return was a foregone conclusion. Whatever his fears for the future and his apprehension at his own weakness, he was willing to answer the call. He wrote to Farel,

As to my intended course of proceeding, this is my present feeling: had I the choice at my own disposal, nothing would be less agreeable to me than to follow your advice. But when I remember that I am not my own, I offer up my heart, presented as a sacrifice to the Lord. Therefore, there is no ground for your apprehension that you will only get fine words. . . . Although I am not very ingenious, I could easily find excuses to slip neatly out of it and show that it was not my fault. But I am well aware that it is God with whom I have to do, from whose sight such crafty imaginations cannot be hidden. Therefore I submit my will and affections, subdued and held fast, to the obedience of God.

On Tuesday, September 13, 1541, he entered for the second time the city he was to serve for the rest of his life. The Register of the Council contains an entry for that day:

M. Iehan Calvin, minister of the Gospel. The same has arrived from Strassburg and has delivered letters from Strassburg and the pastors there, and also from Basel, which have been read. Afterwards he made, at some length, his excuses for the delay in coming. That done, he prayed that the Church be set in order and a paper drawn up to this effect. And that counselors should be elected to consider this. And, as for him, he offered himself to be always the servant of Geneva.

The Geneva of Calvin's day was, by modern standards, a small town, with no more than thirteen thousand inhabitants—though, as it became a city of refuge to the persecuted, the population was increased between 1549 and 1559 by another five thousand, thus, incidentally, causing a housing problem.

If we want to think of Calvin in his environment, we must imagine a medieval walled city, cut in two by the river Rhône. The two parts, St. Gervais and the city proper, were linked at first by a single wooden bridge which took in the island in the middle; but a smaller stone bridge was begun about 1540. Like old London Bridge, the wooden bridge was a street with a row of houses on each side. From the Isle you looked up on both sides at the houses, many of them turreted, standing among orchards and scattered trees to where on the one hand the Church of St. Gervais and on the other the twin towers of the Cathedral of St. Pierre dominated their surroundings.

Calvin lived in the city itself. After one or two moves, he settled down in 1543 in the house where he was to spend the rest of his life. It was Number Eleven in the Rue des Chanoines—a street at one time occupied, as the name suggests, by the cathedral canons.

Set right in the heart of the city, the Rue des Chanoines led up into the cathedral precincts. Number Eleven was halfway down on the right-hand side going towards the river. Next door at Number Nine had lived, up to 1539, François Bonivard, the famous Prisoner of Chillon—

> *My hair is grey, but not with years,*
> *Nor grew it white*
> *In a single night,*
> *As men's have grown from sudden fears.*

Some time later, it became the home of Michel Cop, son of that Rector of Paris University through whose sermon Calvin was compelled to go into exile.

Calvin's house has been completely altered, but it was probably like most other houses in Geneva—a living room at the front and the kitchen, which was also the dining room, behind it, and the bedrooms upstairs. It must have been comfortably large to house the large family that he brought to it. At the back, a good garden sloped down to the huge sixth-century city wall, and from the house there was a fine view over the lower town to the Jura Mountains on the left, the Alps on the right, and in the middle the Lake bordered by its vineyards and hills. Perhaps he had this view and his own garden in mind when in his *Commentary on Genesis* he writes: "We view the world with our eyes, we tread the earth with our feet, we touch innumerable kinds of God's works with our hands, we smell the sweet and pleasant fragrance of herbs and flowers; we enjoy boundless blessings."

When his friend Monsieur de Fallais, a country gentleman, wanted to take a house in Geneva, he asked Calvin to find him one. In the reply, we not only see something of what Calvin's own house was like, but also have one of the very rare glimpses into his domestic life.

> As for yourself, in obedience to your commission, I have
> looked about since my return for a convenient dwelling.
> As for that at the Clébergue, you would be too far away
> from the neighbors you desire—although I have long had

a hankering after it for myself, to retire there when I want some leisure. They promised to let me have an answer, but none has come. If I had had it at my disposal, as they had given me to hope, you know that it would be very much at your service. Near us, I have not been able to find one with a garden more suitable for you than the one I have taken. Not that I am quite content with it, but I took it for want of a better. You will have in front a small garden and a fairly spacious court. There is another garden at the back. A great drawing-room, with as beautiful a view as you could well desire for the summer. The other rooms have not so pleasant an aspect as I would like. But when you have arrived, perhaps we may devise some satisfactory arrangement. With the exception of the drawing-room, one might find houses better furnished and more conveniently laid out; but there would have been no garden, and that, I see, is a feature you desire most of all. However, it is rented for twelve crowns. If, when you see it, you say that is too much, I shall have my excuse ready, that I am not such a manager as to be very sparing of my purse any more than that of others. I have hurried on the bargain solely on account of the garden. . . . Awaiting your final resolve, we shall sow without making any fuss about it, and also prune the vines.

Here in the Rue des Chanoines, Calvin lived very simply.

There is a legend that a Roman Cardinal who was passing through Geneva *incognito* thought he would pay a visit on this prince of the Protestants. He expected to find him living in a style that would rival the Pope, a palace and surrounded by servants. Instead, when he knocked at the door of that ordinary house, Number Eleven, the door was opened by Calvin himself. This story is probably only a legend, but it is very plain that his state worried him very little. He was insistent that the clerical stipends in Geneva should be sufficient, but he never desired to be rich. We find his views on the matter expressed in the *Commentary on Galatians*:

It is probable that the teachers and ministers of the Word were neglected at that time. This showed the basest ingratitude. How disgraceful it is to defraud of their temporal support those by whom our souls are fed. . . . Though it does not become us to indulge too much in complaint or to be too tenacious of our rights, yet Paul found himself called upon to exhort the Galatians to perform this part of their duty. . . . He saw that the ministers of the Word were neglected because the Word itself was despised; for if the Word be truly esteemed, its ministers will always receive kind and honorable treatment. He does not propose that no limit should be set to the ministers' worldly enjoyments or that they should revel in superfluous abundance, but merely that none of the necessary supports of life should be withheld. Ministers ought to be satisfied with moderate fare, and the danger which attends pomp and luxury ought to be prevented.

His own salary was sufficient for his need. Besides the furnished house rent free, he was allowed five hundred florins a year (six hundred after 1562) and enough corn and wine for his household. It is difficult to translate this into modern currency, but we may notice that it was more than the other ministers received, but no more than his additional expenses demanded. At one time he asked for his salary to be reduced to bring it into line with that of his colleagues, but the Council would not hear of it. It is enough to say that he lived without financial worry, but he did not get rich at Geneva's expense.

The inhabitants of Number Eleven formed more than a family. They were almost a colony. In the first place, there was Calvin's wife. For during his exile in Strassburg, he had married. Theirs had been no Héloise and Abelard courtship, however. Romantic love, like poetry, seems to have had no place in his character. Yet the prosaic wooing led to a happy marriage.

It all began with Farel and Bucer being seized with the matchmaking zeal so common in the happily married, who would have all men as themselves. Calvin, who looked upon their relationship to him as almost parental, was forced to take the matter seriously. But he made very clear to Farel the sort of wife he wanted: "Always keep in mind what I seek to find in her; for I am not one of those insane lovers who embrace even the vices of those they are in love with, when they are smitten at first sight with a fine figure. The only beauty which allures me is this—that she be chaste, not too nice or fastidious, economical, patient, likely to take care of my health."

Soon a bride was suggested. But Calvin would have none of her. She knew no French and, as she was of noble birth, he was afraid "she might be too mindful of her family and education." Negotiations were begun with another, who was well spoken of, and went so smoothly that Calvin invited Farel to the wedding, fixed provisionally for the first week in March 1540. But when June came he was still unmarried, and, what was more, was writing to Farel: "I have not yet found a wife, and frequently hesitate as to whether I ought any more to seek one. Claude and my brother had lately betrothed me to a demoiselle. Three days after they had returned, some things were told me which forced me to send my brother to discharge us from that obligation."

Two months later, he had taken matters into his own hands and had married Idelette de Bure, a widow with two children, Jacques and Judith. Her husband, a Frenchman, had been an Anabaptist, and is said to have been converted to the Reformed faith through Calvin. However that may be, she and Calvin were married in August 1540. He does not say much about her in his letters during the eight and a half years of their married life. Only now and then does a remark show how close they were to one another. In the spring of 1541, Strassburg was ravaged by the plague. Calvin stayed in the city but sent his wife away. He wrote to Farel telling him his troubles: "To the bitterness of grief, therefore, has been added great anxiety for those who have survived. Day and night my wife has been constantly in my thoughts, in need of advice now that she is separated from her husband."

During their first summer back in Geneva, she had a son prematurely. A month later Calvin was replying to Viret's friendly enquiries:

> My wife returns her thanks to yours for so much kind and godly comfort. She is unable to reply, except by an amanuensis, and it would be difficult for her even to dictate a letter. The Lord has certainly inflicted a severe and bitter wound in the death of our baby son. But He is Himself a Father and knows best what is good for His children.

They had no more children, and she was never really well again. She died in the spring of 1549. It was again to Viret that Calvin unburdened his heart:

> You know well how tender, or rather soft, my mind is. Had not a powerful self-control been given to me, I could not have borne up so long. And truly, mine is no common source of grief. I have been bereaved of the best companion of my life, of one who, had it been so ordained, would have willingly shared not only my poverty but even my death. During her life she was the faithful helper of my ministry. From her I never experienced the slightest hindrance. She was never troublesome to me throughout the whole course of her illness, but was more anxious about her children than about herself. As I feared these private worries might upset her to no purpose, I took occasion three days before she died, to mention that I would not fail in discharging my duty towards her children.

With Calvin, his wife, and her daughter (for the son seems to have stayed behind in Strassburg), there lived also Calvin's younger brother Antoine and his wife and children. Antoine had shared his brother's fortune since 1536 when they and their sister Marie left Paris for the last time and set out for Strassburg, only to be detained in Geneva. He went into exile with him in 1538, working with him in Strassburg and returning to Geneva with him. They were inseparable. But his life and that of the whole household was clouded by his wife's adultery. She had been imprisoned on suspicion of adultery in 1548, but soon released. The crash came nine years later. She was convicted of adultery with Calvin's own manservant. Antoine divorced her, and she was exiled from Geneva, leaving him with four children, Samuel and David, Anne and Suzanne. Three years later he married again, and once again had four children.

It is strange to realize that for most of his life Calvin's house was full of young children. No doubt the womenfolk protected both him and the children from one another, but at any rate he passed his life, not in the seclusion of a monastery or in humanistic quiet but in the midst of the pleasures and worries of domesticity. The *Institutes* was not written in an ivory tower, but against the background of teething troubles.

His days were filled with work, from the hour when the great bell of St. Pierre, the *Réveille-matin*, called the family to its daily tasks until the end of the day and, often enough, far into the night. Nicholas Colladon, his biographer, looks back upon his travails with amazement:

> If we come to consider his work, I do not believe there can be found his like. For who could recount his ordinary and extraordinary labors? I doubt if any man in our time has had more to listen to, to reply to, to write, or things of greater importance. The multitude and quality alone of his writings is enough to astonish everyone who looks at them, and still more those who read them. . . . He never ceased working, day and night, in the service of the Lord, and heard most unwillingly the prayers and exhortations that his friends were daily addressing to him that he should give himself some rest. Even in his last illness he only stopped dictating about eight hours before he died, his voice at last playing him traitor. Beside the innumerable cares belonging to his pastorate, Calvin had to bear the heaviest load in all the difficulties and perils that this poor city found itself in, assailed within by several mutinous and desperate citizens, tormented without in a thousand ways, menaced by the greatest kings and princes of Christendom.

Not that his life was without any recreation or lacked its lighter moments. His amusements were largely intellectual, and lay in books and conversation—though, so far as that goes, what Dr. Johnson said of John Wesley was true also of him: "John Wesley's conversation is good, but he is never at leisure." A public man who also writes enough to fill fifty quarto volumes in half as many years may be forgiven if he has little leisure. Once or twice while he was at Geneva, he allowed himself a holiday and went to stay at a cottage on the shores of the lake that Antoine had bought in 1553.

Sometimes his letters will disclose amusing incidents, as in the merry affair of the apples. Master Alberg was a confidence trickster, something of an Autolycus. Calvin tells Oswalk Myconius,

> You must understand that this person has for many years been engaged in nothing else but constantly running about from one place to another, to shuffle money out of

some, clothes from others, and thus living from hand to mouth, maintaining a livelihood by imposture, as is the wont of these wandering vagabonds. . . . Afterwards he came to Strassburg, where he extorted twenty batzen from me, which I myself was obliged to borrow from someone else, for I had sold my books and was then entirely without funds. He had promised that he would return the money in a few days. He deposited a valueless box with me as a pledge. He returned some months later, laughing up his sleeve (or rather making a game of it) and asked whether I would let him have some crowns as a loan. I replied that I needed the small sum he had already got. In the meantime, the rascal took the box away out of my library by stealth to consign it to the care of Bucer's wife. She would have nothing to do with it, and told me about it. Thereupon I reprimanded his impudence before several witnesses. Six months, or perhaps a year, later he coolly wrote to me that he was shut up in Baden, that all the gentry of the district were in league against him, and that he could not escape unless I sent a travelling merchant to bring him away in his basket of goods! . . . We had a laugh over this. . . . As I knew the little box contained many trifles of no value I opened it in the presence of many witnesses. It contained mouldy apples, and all sorts of trash, some books tattered and torn, and these quite commonplace, such as Despauterius [a school textbook] and the like. I found also a letter which he had surreptitiously carried off from me. This Sturm was well aware of, whom I called to be present. We replaced everything, with a good deal of laughter.

He was a rogue, but plainly Calvin liked him.

It is strange that the picture of Calvin that has come down to us is of a cold, severe man, restrained in his emotions and vindictive in his enmities. The man who meets us in his letters and in the accounts of those who knew him is quite different. Reserved he certainly was, but not cold. Hasty and impatient, but not vindictive. Sensitive, easily wounded, highly strung. From this comes his chief fault as a man. His temper, sharp by nature, was irritated by circumstance. We should remember what he had to contend with—his sickness, and particularly his migraine, the distraction and worry of work for which he was by nature unfitted, and the bitter enmity that his church program provoked in Geneva. But the fact remains, his friend Colladon says frankly that towards the end of his life he was "peevish and difficult":

> Others have found him to choleric. I do not want to make a man into an angel. . . . Besides his own natural inclination to anger, his amazingly quick wit, the imprudence of many, the infinite multitude and variety of church affairs, and at the end of his life, his illnesses—both his usual ones and also the more serious —made him peevish and difficult.

But, he goes on to say, Calvin was aware of this fault and fought against it. Sometimes, especially in his younger days, he would fly into a terrible rage, finding vent for his feelings in angry, bitter words and even tears. There was the time in Strassburg in 1539 when Bucer and his fellow pastors distrusted his assurances that he was an orthodox Trinitarian and required him to subscribe to a confession of faith. He poured out his troubles to Farel:

> I sinned grievously in not having been able to keep within bounds; for the bile had taken such complete possession of my mind that I poured out bitterness on all sides. . . . In the conclusion of my speech, I stated my resolution to die rather than to subscribe. Thereupon there was so much fervor on both sides that I could not have been more rude to Caroli himself had he been present. At last I forced myself out of the supper room; but Bucer followed me and when he had calmed me down with fair words he led me back to the rest. . . . When I got home I was seized with an extraordinary paroxysm and found no other comfort than in sighs and tears.

And he tells Farel, to whom he was ever wont to state his mind bluntly, that if he had been present, "I would have poured upon you the whole of the fury that I poured out on others."

After these fits of passion would come nervous trouble. Normally abstemious in his food, and taking for many years only one meal a day, he would on these occasions overeat, gobbling his meal furiously. That brought on severe attacks of indigestion and his headaches. It is a remarkable fact, however, that in spite of this trait in his character, he had a way of making and keeping friends. Those close friends who dropped away from him, Louis du Tillet in his early days, and de Fallais later on, did so because they remained or became Romanists. But many of his friendships were lifelong. Three of his friends in Geneva at least he had known since his student days. Mathurin Cordier, his Latin tutor at Paris, came later on to Geneva to be Rector of the Academy there. Michel Cop of Paris came to live next door to him. Theodore Beza, closest of all to him in his closing years, had lived in the same house with him at Bourges.

　　The reason for his rich friendship is not far to seek. People knew just where they stood with him. Deceit was utterly foreign to his nature. When his friends were wrong, he told them so without mincing matters, and the closer the friend, the blunter his criticisms. Farel chafed under this plainness, but got only the reply: "I entreat you, my dear brother, when I expostulate with you, chide you, get warm with you, accuse you, that you take it all the same as if you were dealing thus with yourself."

　　It was just because he was unswerving in his devotion to God that he was such a good friend. He could be severe: When Farel as an old man married, in somewhat dubious circumstances, a young girl, Calvin refused to have anything more to do with him (though on his deathbed he forgave him, wrote to him, and they met once more). But on the other hand, he would give himself any trouble to help someone. It might be one of his friends' relatives sick of the plague; he would visit him, regardless of his own safety. It might be an old woman who did not want to be left in Strassburg when her pastor had gone back to Geneva; he wrote to Viret to find her a house in the city. It may be a sick man that he sends to his good friend the manager of the hospital. His friends knew that there was more in him than peevishness and difficulty.

　　For his part, he was a man who could not live without friendship and was dependent on the kindness of others. He wrote pathetically to Farel: "I beg and entreat you to alleviate the irksomeness of my present situation with long and frequent letters; for unless my weariness can be refreshed by the comfort of friendship, I shall be utterly in darkness."

CHAPTER 6

# MINISTER OF THE WORD OF GOD

"I felt as if God had laid his mighty hand upon me," said Calvin after Farel had adjured him to work in Geneva. He believed that God had called him there, and although, when he was asked to return from Strassburg, he was at first an unwilling prophet, his consent to go back was an act of obedience to God's call. He would not otherwise have gone. This call alone justified his ministry and his sufferings and gave him the courage to strive to realize the idea of the Church that he believed to find in the New Testament and the early Church.

We may refresh our minds as to what his work in Geneva was. In church history books or lives of Calvin, he is shown, often as not, simply as an ecclesiastical politician or statesman. We are told (quite properly) that he worked out from Ephesians 4:11–13 a doctrine of the Church upon which he sought to build the Church in Geneva. But when his work is thought of in this doctrinaire way, it bears as little resemblance to his real aims and struggles as a stuffed seagull in a glass case does to the living bird that delights us with its freedom as it now hangs in the air and now swoops on the wind above a cliff-top.

If we turn to Calvin's comments on Ephesians 4:11–13, we see how we miss the mark if we think of his work primarily in terms of ecclesiastical polity, or a doctrine of the ministry, or an enforcement of discipline.

*And he gave some, apostles: and some, prophets: and some, evangelists: and some, pastors, and teachers: for the perfecting of the saints, for the work of the ministry, for the edifying of the body of Christ: till we all come in the unity of the faith, and of the knowledge of the Son of God, onto a perfect man, onto the measure of the stature of the fullness of Christ. (Eph. 4:11–13)*

Calvin comments:

The government of the Church by the preaching of the Word is first of all declared to be no human contrivance, but a most sacred ordinance of Christ. The apostles did not appoint themselves, but were chosen by Christ; and at the present day, ministers do not rashly thrust themselves forward by their own judgment, but are raised up by the Lord. In short, the government of the Church by the ministry of the Word is not a contrivance of men, but an appointment made by the Son of God. As His own unalterable law, it demands our assent. They who reject or despise this ministry offer insult and rebellion to Christ its author. It is Himself who gave them; for, if he does not raise them up, there will be none. . . . To Christ we owe it that we have ministers of the gospel, that they abound in necessary qualifications, that they execute the trust committed to them. All, all is His gift.

Our true completeness and perfection consists in our being united in the one body of Christ. No language that more highly commends the ministry of the Word could have been employed, than to ascribe to it this effect. What is more excellent than to produce the true and complete perfection of the Church? And yet this work, so admirable and divine, is here declared to be accomplished by the external ministry of the Word. That those who neglect this instrument should hope to become perfect in Christ is sheer madness. . . . This is the universal rule, which applies equally to the highest and the lowest. The Church is the common mother of all the godly, bearing, nourishing and bringing up children to God, kings and peasants alike: and this is done by the ministry.

Here the preaching of the Word of God is central. It is by the preaching of the gospel that God forms, builds, and rules His Church. This is as true for Geneva in the sixteenth century as for Jerusalem or Galatia in the first. Therefore, the primary and central work of the Church in Geneva was the proclaiming of the Word of God. This belief is embodied in the famous *Ordinances of the Church in Geneva.*

When Calvin returned from exile, he at once asked for a committee of pastors and laymen to be set up to prepare a constitution for the Church. The *Ordinances* which they drew up were, after some opposition, accepted by the Councils. There are, says this document, four offices in the Church: pastors, doctors, elders, and deacons. The work of the pastors is "to proclaim the Word of God so as to teach, admonish, exhort and reprove both in public and in private, to administer the sacraments and, with the elders, to make brotherly corrections." The doctors are "to instruct believers in wholesome doctrine, so that the purity of the gospel shall not be adulterated by ignorance or false opinions." To the elders is committed the task of "taking care of the life of each person, admonishing them lovingly when they see them at fault or leading a disorderly life; and they shall make a report to the body that shall be deputed to make brotherly corrections." The deacons have the oversight of the poor and the sick. All these are not unrelated activities of the Church, but different manifestations of the Church's service of the Word of God.

Calvin was not only the architect of the Church in Geneva, bearing, as the leading pastor, the chief responsibility for the Church's life and organization, but he was also actively engaged in the pastoral work. Undoubtedly, he looked upon his life work in Geneva primarily as "proclaiming the Word of God" and "instructing believers in wholesome doctrine." His time was not spent in sitting in an office and planning, nor was it devoted entirely to committees. He was a pastor, busied with the common run of pastoral duties. For example, glancing through the Annals of Geneva, we find that on November 5, 1553, he married two couples in the Cathedral; that on December 10 of the same year he "blessed a marriage and administered baptism at St. Pierre." The first quarter of 1554 kept him busy: on January 7, he had a marriage at St. Pierre, on January 28 two, two more on February 4, three on February 18, one on March 4, and a baptism on March 18, and three marriages on April 1. All in all, for the ten years 1550–1559 for which we have a register, he took about two hundred and seventy weddings and fifty baptisms.

There seems to have been no regular house-to-house visiting by the pastors, but only visits to those who were sick or in some trouble. Calvin undertook this duty also. When the plague came to Geneva in 1542 the Council is said to have forbidden him to visit its victims. But he tells Viret that he is ready to take the place of the minister Peter Blanchet if he should fall sick:

> The pestilence begins to rage here with greater violence, and few who are at all affected by it escape its ravages. One

of our colleagues had to be set apart for visiting the sick. Because Peter offered himself everyone readily agreed! If anything happens to him, I am afraid I must take the risk upon myself since, as you say, we must not fail those who stand in more need of our ministry than any others. And yet it is not my opinion that, while we want to provide for one part, we are free to neglect the whole body of the Church. But so long as we are in this ministry, I do not see that any excuse will avail us if, through fear of infection, we are found wanting in the discharge of our duty where we are most needed.

But the center of his pastoral work, around which all else resolved, was the preaching of the gospel. By this means, Calvin says time and again, God reveals Himself in His judgment and mercy, turning hearts to obedience, confirming the faith of believers, building up and purifying the Church.

Under the *Ordinances*, each Sunday began with its service and sermon at daybreak (six o'clock in summer and seven in winter) and went on with catechism for the children at midday and another sermon at three o'clock. Sermons were fixed for Monday, Tuesday, and Friday mornings until in 1549 when they were increased to every day of the week. Calvin's special charge was St. Pierre, where his custom was to preach twice every Sunday and once every day of alternate weeks.

His method was that of Zwingli and some of the Church fathers. Not for him the single text or even the isolated passage, he preached steadily through book after book of the Bible. On Sundays, he took always the New Testament, except for a few Psalms on Sunday afternoons. During the week, apart from occasional high festivals, it was always the Old Testament. He began at the beginning of a book and expounded it passage by passage, clause by clause, day after day, until he came to the end. Then he started on another book.

Thanks chiefly to two men, we have a detailed picture of his preaching from 1549 until his death. The group of French refugees in Geneva who had banded together as the "Company of Foreigners" prized Calvin highly as their father in God. "Seeing the great profit that would result from his sermons being taken down in writing," says Colladon, "they tried to find a man who was a skilful, quick writer, and whom they would pay such wages as they were able." They were fortunate in finding one of their own number, a poor man with a family to support. He, Denis Raguenier, took down the sermons in shorthand and wrote them out afterwards in bound volumes for people to borrow and study at their leisure. It is due to him that we have a thousand or more sermons still remaining.

The details of order and dates are filled in for us by Nicholas Colladon. On Sunday, August 25, 1549, Calvin began to preach on Acts, and continued with it until March 1554. On weekdays during this while, he had preached on eight of the minor Prophets and on Daniel, Lamentations, and Ezekiel. After Acts, he went on to both epistles to the Thessalonians, both to the Corinthians, the three Pastoral Epistles, Galatians, and Ephesians. This made up his Sunday preaching until May 1558. Then comes a gap while he was very ill during the winter of 1558–1559. Spring found him better again, and Colladon records his first sermon:

> It was a great joy to the whole Church when he first entered the pulpit after his illness. I remember it was a Sunday, and we sang Psalm 30, which was just right for giving thanks for his recovery. We could see by his face with what a real piety he gave thanks to God.

At this point, he took up the Harmony of the Gospels and had not completed the series at his death. But on weekdays of all this time, he had preached through Job, Deuteronomy, Isaiah, Genesis, Judges, both books of Samuel, and both of Kings.

Calvin had a very good reason for this monumental preaching. If we remember how he thought of the Bible as the Word of God where our Creator and Redeemer meets with us, we can understand how he wanted to bring the whole message of the Bible before his people. This could be done in more than one way—by using the epistle and gospel for the day, for instance, as Luther did. But to Calvin's mind it could best be done by connected exposition. And without doubt, this gave a great breadth to his preaching. No single idea and no one line of thought was pursued exclusively. By expounding Scripture as a whole he was forced to deal with the Scriptural range of ideas. And, as an honest interpreter, he labored to represent the thought of the Bible faithfully. He had a horror of those who preached their own ideas in place of the gospel of the Bible: "When we enter the pulpit, it is not so that we may bring our own dreams and fancies with us."

But, on the other hand, the preacher's task is not simply to repeat Bible ideas in Bible language. He must explain what the Bible means and apply its teaching to the congregation before him. He must seek to destroy the barriers that the centuries have built up, so that the passage may sound as freshly and relevantly to the congregation in St. Pierre in the sixteenth century as it had done to its first hearers long before. Part of his preaching is, of course, general—applying the Bible's words of judgment, comfort, and exhortation to his people's hearts in a devotional way. The basic needs of men are the same in the sixteenth century as in the first century A.D. or the eighth B.C. But when occasion requires, he will speak directly on a topical issue:

> When elections have to be made, just as today the gover-
> nors have to be elected, and tomorrow and the day after
> and throughout the week the estates of this city and the
> judicial order have to be provided for, how many are there
> who think of God when they undertake this, which is such
> a religious thing? The most solemn of all the elections is
> due now—but those who will come to it, where are they,
> most of them? I met some of my bumpkins (I could easily
> point them out by name, but there is no need, for we all
> know them well enough); some of them were going up to
> the Bourg de four, and others were coming this way. They
> thought they would have no time for breakfast unless they
> chose service time. I saw this with my own eyes as I was
> coming to church. And is it not a crying shame? So when
> it is plain that we who ought to be well learned in the
> Word of God, seeing it is preached to us intimately every
> day, are still so stupid—more, that we have such a spirit of
> brutishness in us—is not this a great shame? Now then, let
> us consider that we are not told without good reason that,
> when we are going to elect men to some public position,
> we must set about it reverently and carefully. For we shall
> provoke God's anger if we pollute the seat of justice, put-
> ting men in it who have neither the zeal nor the interest
> to honor and serve it. And so our present circumstances
> show us that, since St. Paul recommended the election of
> widows, we must learn (if we do not want to spoil every-

thing) to do better than we have done so far, to be really serious and take care when elections have to be made, so that God may reign among us and that He may bring it to pass that all are governed by His Holy Spirit and that they may have zeal and love for His Word.

We might imagine ourselves making one in that congregation. We are, shall we say, refugees from England in the reign of Mary. The great Gothic Cathedral of St. Pierre is well filled. This, however, not for the preacher's fame, but because it is an offense in Geneva to absent oneself from worship. Some of our fellows in the congregation, therefore, are little interested in the sermon, perhaps sigh for the colorful spectacle of the Mass that is no more. Nor does the preacher set out to interest them, for he has no amusing or startling anecdotes to take their fancy and hold their interest, like Hugh Latimer whom we have heard preach in St. Edward's Church in Cambridge. But a large part of the congregation needs no such aids: We see about us the devout Genevans themselves, the many refugees like ourselves from England, Scotland, and from France, and the group of Italian nobles who have left their homes, possessions, and honors to worship God "purely"; and there sits Denis Raguenier taking down every word—no difficult task while the asthma-stricken creature gasps between sentences to recover his breath.

Calvin has reached his fiftieth sermon on I Timothy. The passage for this morning is chapter 6, verses 12–14: "Fight the good fight of faith, lay hold on eternal life, whereunto thou art called, and hast made a good confession before many witnesses. I charge thee in the sight of God who quickeneth all things, and before Jesus Christ who witnessed a good confession before Pontius Pilate that thou keep this commandment." He reminds us of what he had said this morning, that we must persevere patiently in our Christian life. "But since the patience of believers is of great extent and comprises many parts, St. Paul has declared his meaning more plainly by adding that we must fight—as if we were saying that faith cannot exist without conflict. Whoever wants his service to be approved by God, must get ready for battle, for we have an enemy who never slackens."

But why can faith never exist without conflict? In the first place, there are many hindrances from outside that make us turn aside or stumble.

Even if a Christian man did not go outside himself he would still need to fight to persist in the faith. For it is a fact that there is nothing more contrary to our nature than to leave earthly things and not be devoted to them but to seek with all our heart and understanding that which is invisible, entirely hidden from our eyes and entirely incomprehensible to our senses. A Christian man must rise above himself when it is a question of thinking of the kingdom of God and everlasting life. But, nevertheless, we know how our spirits are inclined to what we grasp in our hand. How then will it be possible for us to persist in the faith unless we do violence to our whole nature?

Yet this is a good fight, not doubtful in the outcome like all human wars but blessed in the end and good for those who undertake it.

So then we must bear in mind the three steps St. Paul puts here. The first is that faith cannot be without many assaults, and that the life of the children of God is like a warfare in this world. The second is that we must not be upset if God tries us, for we are not fighting at a venture, nor in danger of losing our life irrevocably or of being despoiled of our goods and position: but the issue of our warfare is much to be longed for, seeing that God rules over us, that it is He who calls us, and He does not want our time to be wasted. And moreover, let us know for the third, that God is not satisfied with rewarding us in this world, but He sets before us something much more excellent—the inheritance of the kingdom of heaven. Seeing, then, that He wishes us to pass through this world in order to come to Him and to enjoy for ever His glory and everlasting blessedness, which He has bought for us so dearly by the blood of our Lord Jesus Christ, is it not proper that each of us should apply himself wholly to that? And then, are we held fast in this world by visible things? When we compare the heavenly life with all that is desirable in this world, I ask you, although the honors, the riches, the goods, the delights and all those things to which men devote themselves, are pleasing to us, must they not become like dung and refuse when we are concerned with the glory of God?

We must remember, however, that it is beyond our own strength to start on this heavenly life, just as it is beyond our power to win through to a successful conclusion. We are not saved by our own industry but are called to everlasting life by God. Certainly, when we are called, we must lay hold on eternal life. We must take pains and strive. But all the same, it is purely of God's free goodness that we are saved.

> God does not want us to be idle, but yet it is with fear and trembling. And why? Because it is God who works in us, giving us the will, giving us the result, and the whole thing according to His good pleasure. Let us strive to the utmost of our ability, but without presumption, without pride. Let us not think of doing well to get merits, nor as if man were worthy to be exalted over against God, for thus the grace of God would be obscured, even entirely annihilated.

Moreover, this battle is lifelong. It is no good for us to begin well and then grow weary and not continue. This would be the basest ingratitude, considering the greatness of the blessing to which God has called us.

> We might say, "I have done this, and I have done that; is it not enough?" What? What are the terms upon which God has called us to His service? Is it just for one act, or two, and that thereafter He has given us leave to have a rest? Not at all; it is that we may dedicate ourselves to Him in life and in death, and that we may be His entirely.

But some people think that if, as they pretend, they have fought valiantly in time past, they can now do what they like, living on their reputation. If they were angels in paradise, they could still not plead that as an excuse. If we have confessed Jesus Christ before witnesses, perhaps have led our neighbors to a good life, we are doubly bound to continue, for our sake and for theirs. If we fail, in doctrine or in life, we shall be held responsible if those who have seen and profited by our good confession in the past are hurt. Yet, once again, it is as much beyond our power to continue as it is to begin; we must therefore pray to God to give us strength to go on.

> We see a great number whose heart fails them when they see that the work is greater than their strength: "Oh," they say, "how shall I be able to do that? I feel that I am so weak and I can see that is a great burden and beyond my bearing." No, no; let us just work, however difficult things may be, and God will work for us. And since St. Paul in talking of things that surpass the strength of men never fails to exhort them to do them, we must understand that it is no excuse to plead that we have been shocked and dismayed because we see that we are unable to bear the burden that God lays upon our shoulders; for He knows what we can do—nothing at all. And moreover, He will not fail us while we walk in humility, and undertake to subject ourselves to Him and to put ourselves entirely in His hands.

Now the preacher is drawing to the end:

> Let us then look upon the life that God keeps hidden in Himself and which He has manifested when He revealed it by His Holy Spirit, and of which He has given a good testimony in His gospel. When the world, then, shall have conspired our death a hundred thousand times, so that we are regarded as damnable and held despicable, let us mount above it, for our life is not here below, it does not depend on men or their credit or good opinion; don't let us overrate all that, but rise above all the vexations that the devil puts before us to weaken our courage, because we know that it is God who quickens all things. He holds our life in His hands, He will take good and safe care of it; and what is more, He wants us to strain towards Him, that we may be content with knowing that He will not defraud us of what He has promised to us. . . . In the midst of death we can hope for life, knowing that nothing can make us fall when the unconquerable power of God protects us, that those who molest us today shall finish in confusion

and that in the end God will make us to triumph with our
Lord Jesus Christ.

Such preaching as this, pursued so regularly and applied so stringently to
the people, was the central explosive point of the Church's work in Geneva. It was made even more powerful by the exercise of the discipline.
The discipline ought not to be confused with the civil laws of Geneva
which regulated the private lives of the citizens, though, plainly enough,
the two often overlapped—for breaking the civil law would sometimes in-
volve breaking the Law of God. The medieval Church had exercised its
pastoral discipline by means of confession. Calvin was not willing to abol-
ish confession without substituting another form of discipline. He explains
to Farel the form of discipline that he is exercising in his French Church
in Strassburg:

> I have often declared to you that it did not seem expedient
> to me that confession should be abolished in the churches
> unless that which I have lately taught be substituted for it.
> So that I may explain my method to you the better, let me
> first of all state the true nature of the case. When the day
> of the sacrament of the Supper draws near, I give notice
> from the pulpit that those who are desirous of communi-
> cating must first of all let me know; at the same time, I add
> for what purpose—that those who are as yet uninstructed
> and inexperienced in religion may be better trained and
> that those who need special admonition may get it, and
> lastly that if there are any suffering under trouble of mind
> they may receive comfort.

This is quite a mild form of discipline, not much different from that of the
English Prayer Book. In Geneva, however, Calvin was able to go further
by developing the same idea and by coming closer to what he taught in the
*Institutes*. There he says that every kind of society needs its own discipline
and the Church no less:

> For what will be the consequence if every man be at lib-
> erty to follow his own inclinations? But such would be the
> case if the preaching of the doctrine were not accompa-

nied by private admonitions, reproofs and other methods to enforce the doctrine and prevent it from being altogether ineffectual. Discipline serves, therefore, as a bridal to curb and restrain the refractory who resist the doctrine of Christ, or as a spur to stimulate the inactive, and sometimes as a father's rod, with which those who have grievously fallen may be chastised in mercy and with a gentleness of the Spirit of Christ.

We shall see in the next chapter how this was put into practice in Geneva. But for the moment, we may observe that here we have no doctrinaire scheme of church planning, as Richard Hooker tried to make out in his famous account of Calvin's work in the Preface to the Ecclesiastical polity, but a sincere attempt to bring the gospel into the closest possible connection with the lives of the people. Discipline was a pastoral measure, a part of the proclamation of the Word of God.

# CHAPTER 7

# THE CONFLICT OF THE WORD

The struggles that the militant Church is engaged in are rarely clear-cut in their issues. They do not often appear as a battle between Christ and anti-Christ. Standing outside them or viewing them over a distance of the years, we can see what was at stake and can simplify them into one of the battles in the war of the Word of God. But even so, to many spectators of the world, it seems as if this is a struggle for something quite different and that the Church is behaving in a self-conscious and hysterical way.

The ostensible issue may be some practical matter that seems to have little or nothing to do with the "real" work of the Church. It may be that the Church insists on relating her gospel to the life of the world by pronouncing on a political question or drawing attention to some social evil, or that she not only preaches the gospel but seeks to embody it consistently in her practical life. For example, what was the riot at Ephesus about in Acts 19? Was it simply a question of economics, as Demetrius and his fellow silversmiths held, or was the freedom of the Word of God at stake? Or again, most of the issues involved in the conflict of the Church with the Nazis in various countries were practical ones, like the persecution of the Jews, or the sterilization of the mentally unsound, or the education of the young.

But in these practical matters the Church believed she was fighting for Christ and His Gospel. We may also notice that the opponent will try to hide the religious significance of the struggle, making it out to be not a matter of principle but purely practical, and exhorting the Church, with considerable righteousness, to keep to the task of preaching the gospel and caring for souls. So long as the Church stays indoors and preaches and worships quietly in her small corner, she will be left in peace. But when she affects private lives and vested interests, here (as Richard Hooker said about something quite different) "is the boil that will not be touched."

The conflict in Geneva followed this pattern. Calvin's preaching, pointed and barbed as it was, could not fail to offend many. But the preaching by itself would hardly have provoked such opposition if it had not impinged directly upon the lives of the citizens through the exercise of discipline in the Church, and it was on a practical point in connection with the discipline that the main struggle was fought.

In the *Ordinances* of 1541, the duty of excommunicating the impenitent was placed with the Consistory, the church court consisting of the ministers and twelve elders. Although the Council had accepted this position in theory, they were unwilling to allow it in practice. They looked upon it from a political point of view and were afraid for the Church to possess what seemed to them a powerful political weapon. In the Middle Ages, the ban of the Church had been a force that even the strongest rulers had had to reckon with. Calvin's thought, however, was moving on a different plane altogether. What was at stake for him was, in the first resort, the autonomy of the Church, and ultimately, the Lordship of Christ over the Church. Thus, for example, he would not allow any jurisdiction over the Church's doctrine to the Senate of Berne, and with passion writes to Viret, who was there at the time:

> As to the mode of procedure, this point ought to be weighed carefully, what a fatal precedent they are going to set if the brethren acknowledge the Senate as a judge in regard to doctrine, so that whatever the Senate sanctions must be accepted and embraced by us as if proceeding from an oracle. What kind of a precedent, and how great a pre-judgment must this be for posterity! Assuredly, if we let the yoke be imposed upon us like this, we treacherously betray the sacred ministry by our dissimulation.

And what he will not permit in regard to doctrine, he equally forbids for worship (we recall that it was for this cause that he was exiled in 1538) and also for discipline.

The State and the Church each has its own sphere in government committed to it by God, and neither may take to itself the jurisdiction of the other. There is, Calvin says in the *Institutes* in the section on discipline, a great distinction

> between the ecclesiastical and the civil power. For the Church has no power of the sword to punish or to coerce, no authority to compel, no prisons, fines or other punishments, like those inflicted by the civil magistrate. Besides, the object of this power is, not that he who has trans-

gressed may be punished against his will but that he may profess his repentance by a voluntary submission to chastisement. The difference therefore is very great; because the Church does not assume to itself what belongs to the magistrate, nor can the magistrate execute that which is executed by the Church. This will be better understood by an example. Is any man drunk? In a well-regulated city he will be punished by imprisonment. Has he committed fornication? He will receive the same or a severer punishment. With this the laws, the magistrate and the civil judgment will all be satisfied; though it may be that he will give no sign of repentance, but will rather murmur and repine against his punishment. Will the Church stop here? Such persons cannot be admitted to the sacred Supper without doing an injury to Christ and to His holy institution. And reason requires that he who has offended the Church by an evil example should remove, by a solemn declaration of repentance, the offense which he has excited.

When, therefore, the Genevan Senate claimed the right of excommunication, he resisted with might and main.

In spite of the assurances that had been given him that things would be different this time, Calvin had not long been back before opposition broke out afresh. Some who had been foremost in freeing Geneva from the Roman yoke found that the Reformation was not what they had hoped. It was on the side of order, not turbulence, and there were not wanting lusty young blades whom this irked. But especially the high moral standard that Calvin was insisting on went against the grain.

The old and happy days of fighting and whoring, or, for the more respectable, dicing and dancing, were over. Geneva had become a religious town. The Councils had passed laws regulating the lives of the citizens. Worse, the ministers were inciting the Councils to enforce the laws. Nobody minded having these rules; they were common to every European city in the sixteenth century. What was so unpleasant was that they should be enforced with any degree of rigor and consistency. A few even of the friends of the Reformation began to cool off. Some patrician families were not slow to ask why a Frenchman should occupy such a position of trust and authority in their Church. Unpleasant incidents began to occur. The

Cathedral was disturbed by brawling during services. Guns were fired off outside the door. Calvin himself was not free from insult. As yet, however, there was no organized opposition, and the Councils were, in the main, friendly. What was heard now was largely the murmuring of the disaffected.

But before many years were out, an opposition party, which became known as the Libertines, began to form. It crystallized around a group of aristocrats, particularly the family of Favre and its connections, a dissolute and lawless set. The daughter was married to Ami Perrin, Captain General in Geneva, and formerly a friend of Calvin's, who aptly called the bombastic man "our Caesar" and his terrible Amazon of a wife "Penthesilea." The first real trouble came when Perrin and another of the Senate, Corna, broke the laws of the city by dancing at a wedding. They were imprisoned. On their release, Corna behaved well, acknowledging his fault, but Perrin took it badly. Calvin was alive to the gravity of a breach between himself and the Captain General, and wrote to him in an attempt at reconciliation, but with the utmost frankness:

> You yourself know, or at least ought to know, what I am; that at all events, I am one to whom the law of my heavenly Master is so dear that the cause of no man on earth will induce me to flinch from maintaining it with a pure conscience. I cannot believe that you yourself have any other end in view, but I observe that no one has his eyes open wide enough when he is himself concerned. As for me, I desire in this matter to consult not only the edification of the Church and your salvation, but also your convenience, name and leisure; for how odious would be the imputation which is likely to fall upon you, that you were apparently free from and unrestrained by the common law to which everyone is subject? It is certainly better, and in accord with my zeal for your welfare, to anticipate the danger than that you should be so branded. I have heard indeed what words have come from your house—that I should take care lest I stir up a smoldering fire, lest what occurred before should happen again, in the course of the seventh year. But these speeches have no weight with me; for I did not return to Geneva either for the sake of leisure

or of gain, nor will it again grieve me to be forced to leave it. The convenience and safety of Church and State made me willing to return; and if measures are now being taken against me alone, I should wish it to be said once for all, to all who think me troublesome, "What you do, do quickly." But yet the unworthy treatment and ingratitude of some parties will not make me fail in my duty, and I will lay aside that devoted attachment to this place only with my last breath—for which I take God to witness. Nor will I ever so far yield to the humors of any other individual, as hereafter to dispense with his personal attendance. These observations do not refer to you but to that member of your family who is nearest to you. Nor do I write them with a view to causing quarrels, but that it may be quite clear with what firmness I am about to proceed, whatever may happen. I am especially desirous of impressing upon you the necessity of earnestly seeking to acquire the primary virtue of obedience to God, and respect for the common order and polity of the Church. May the Lord protect you with His own defense, and discover to you how greatly even the stripes of a sincere friend are to be preferred to the treacherous blandishments of others. Adieu!

> Your attached and sincere brother,
> John Calvin

This letter seemed at first to have gone some way to achieving its purpose. But, if Perrin was pricked by it, the influence of his wife who "rages within doors in a terrible way" (says Calvin) soon drove him into ever more bitter opposition.

Hardly a year was past before the uneasy truce flamed into open war. One Jacques Gruet, an intimate of the Favres and who had been in trouble along with them over the dancing affair, wrote a vulgar and scurrilous placard and left it in the pulpit at St. Pierre. Calvin read it as a direct threat against their preaching, and told Viret that he was "threatening us with death unless we keep quiet." The Council was no less alarmed, regarding the paper as a sign of sedition. Gruet was arrested, and under torture confessed to authorship.

The Libertines had suffered a setback, and while they licked their wounds there was peace. Even a touching reconciliation scene was staged in which Favre and "Penthesilea" shook hands with Calvin. But Ami Perrin was riding for a fall. It came out that he had been engaged in some underhand political business with France which, to the Senate, smelled suspiciously like treason. He was deposed from his offices. But the masses chose to make a hero of him, rising in his support and bursting into the Council Chamber. Fighting broke out, and Calvin, in another street, heard the uproar. He wrote to Viret:

> Numerous confused shouts were heard from that quarter. These meanwhile increased to such a pitch as to afford a sure sign of insurrection. I immediately ran to the place. Things looked frightful. I cast myself into the thickest of the crowds, to the amazement of almost everyone. But the whole mob made a rush towards me. They seized me and dragged me hither and thither lest I should suffer some injury! I called God and men to witness that I had come for the purpose of presenting my body to their swords. I exhorted them, if they intended to shed blood, to begin with me. Even the worthless, but more especially the more respectable part of the crowd, at once grew considerably cooler. At last I was dragged through the midst to the Senate. There fresh fights arose, into the midst of which I threw myself. Everyone is of the opinion that a great and disgraceful carnage was prevented from taking place by my interference. My colleagues, meanwhile, were mixed up with the crowd. I succeeded in getting everyone to sit down quietly. They say that all were exceedingly moved by a long and vehement speech, suitable to the occasion, that I delivered.

The riot intimidated the Senate, however, and soon Perrin was reinstated in his offices—or, as Calvin put it to Farel, "our comic friend Caesar has again donned his socks."

Besides these crises, however, Calvin was being continually harried by his opponents, as he had been for years. In 1545, the Council had, without reference to the ministers, appointed one Jean Trolliet as a pastor.

When he was refused, they tried to saddle Calvin with him as a secretary. This also failed, but they had succeeded in worrying Calvin, and Trolliet was now his lifelong enemy.

A year later a member of the Council, Pierre Ameaux, was brought before his fellow councilors because, says the Register, "It has been revealed that Ameaux has said that M. Calvin is a wicked man and only a Picard, and preaches false doctrine." In the end he was let off with the price of apologizing to Calvin in front of the Council. This again was only a little matter, but it was a distracting vexation and a humiliation to Calvin and his office. He told Farel about this time that hardly a week passed without some trouble. Later on he spoke his mind plainly and strongly in a sermon, and the Council, perhaps with some nervousness, minuted:

> M. Calvin, minister. The same preached today with great anger that the magistracy allows many insolences. It is ordered that he be called to the Council to explain why he preached like this; and if the city has committed some insolence, the Lieutenant must take note of it and see that justice is done.

Two months later, on his thirty-ninth birthday, the Council again took umbrage at his preaching and the ministers were told (just as the German Confessing Church was told by the Third Reich) that they must preach only the gospel and not mix it up with current affairs. This interference was dealt with as faithfully as it deserved. But unfortunately, just at this stage a letter Calvin had written to Viret three years earlier fell into the hands of Trolliet, who was not slow in bringing it before the Council, seeing it contained this passage:

> I perceive how evil-disposed they are, and already I have broken ground upon the subject of the internal state of the city in ten sermons. . . . The Syndics have been appointed—Amy Curtet, Amy Perrin, Domeine Arlot, Jacques de Tortonne. Louis Bernard, Peter Verne and two others have been induced to enter the Senate. They give us good hope of themselves. I know not, however, what we may hope; for under the pretext that Christ reigns, they wish to rule without Christ.

The Council made the most of the opportunity presented in this letter and summoned Calvin to explain and apologize. But Trolliet went one better by circulating a translation of the letter round the town. After a month the Council was graciously pleased to acquit Calvin; but not before they had heard some home truths from the mouth of Farel, who was boiling with wrath and welcomed the chance of being able to say what he thought. What did they think they were doing, he asked them, treating a man like M. Calvin in this sort of way? Calvin was no ordinary mortal but a man of great learning "who has even remonstrated with many like Luther and Melanchthon and others like them." If the roughness of the style of the minutes is any guide, he reduced the Council and its secretary to a state of extreme confusion.

But although the opposition might be temporarily discomfited, although on occasion they might be softened by Calvin's pleas even to a reconciliation, the effect soon wore off and the conflict continued. The Libertines were fighting for their interests as Genevan citizens and against the moral yoke which the ministers laid on the city. It was only to be expected that they would have a considerable following, particularly among the irresponsible and the young. Nor were they over-nice in their methods. From what is know it is clear that Ami Perrin fostered sexual vice, and probably there is much that we do not know—certainly in a notorious case in 1549 the accused, a former friend of Perrin's, was forbidden to speak in his defense, beheaded immediately and the unsavory details hushed up. When we compare Calvin with his Genevan opponents, the judgment of a famous German scholar seems almost an understatement: "without doubt Calvin was, in comparison with his opponents, always morally the superior."

Things went on like this until the fateful years 1553–1554, when two large storms blew up from different quarters and raged simultaneously. The one was the decisive battle with the Libertines; the other (of which they were glad to make use) the Servetus affair.

From time to time, Calvin had been involved in theological disputes within Geneva as well as abroad. He had had trouble with Sebastian Castellio, the warden of the school, who had maintained that the Song of Songs was "a lascivious and obscene poem," and therefore not to be reckoned as inspired Scripture. The doctrine of predestination came under fire. A doctor, Bolsec, who later wrote a scandalous life of him, attacked him on this score. Although he was condemned, he was able to harm Calvin's authority in Geneva as a theologian. Trolliet kept the controversy alive and gained some support from the Council. Calvin had much ado to win from them an admission that "the said book, the *Institutes* is good and holy, and its teaching is the holy doctrine of God; and Calvin is a good and true minister of this city." But what they gave with their right hand they took away with their left by passing a vote of confidence in Trolliet.

But the quarrel with Servetus was on quite a different level, with more far-reaching implications. Michael Servetus was a Spaniard, a brilliant man in more than one direction, a medical doctor, a lawyer, and a theologian. He was an example of one sort of man that the humanistic Renaissance gave birth to. But he should have been born three hundred years later. He would have been happy and quite safe in the free-thinking circles of England in the middle of the nineteenth century. Without going deeply into his theological ideas, we may merely note that his doctrine of the Trinity was unorthodox—so unorthodox as to shock every right-thinking man of his day. He tried to gain support for his opinions among some of the Reformers, Oecolampadius, Bucer, and (his fatal mistake) Calvin. Their paths had passed long before Calvin went to Geneva, but he only began to write to the Reformer in 1545. Calvin fobbed him off, misliking the tone of his letters, and wrote to Farel:

> Servetus lately wrote to me and coupled with his letter a
> long volume of his delirious fancies, with the Thrasonic
> boast that I should see something astonishing and unprec-
> edented. He takes it upon him to come hither, if it be
> agreeable to me. But I am unwilling to pledge my word
> for his safety; for if he comes I shall never let him depart
> alive, providing my authority be of any avail.

Events gave this last sentence a fearful significance, so that the threat (if it was intended as a threat and not simply as a warning to Servetus to keep away) has made the trial and execution of Servetus even more sinister.

In 1553, Servetus published a book setting forth his views, calling it, with an eye to the *Institutio*, the *Restitutio*. And since he wanted to strike a blow at Calvin within Geneva itself, he sent a number of copies to the Genevan bookseller, Robert Estienne, who promptly destroyed them. But this book placed him in the class of wanted men. He was discovered where he was living in France and arrested by the Roman Catholics who imprisoned him at Lyons. Had he not contrived to escape, he would undoubtedly have been burned by them. But escape he did and arrived at Geneva of all places. There he was quickly discovered and brought to trial, Calvin prosecuting him on behalf of the Church. "I hope," he wrote to Farel, "that sentence of death will at least be passed upon him; but I want the severity of the punishment to be mitigated." This may mean either that he desired a more swift and merciful death than the stake for Servetus, or that he hoped the death sentence would be passed but not carried out. Farel seems to have taken him in this latter way and warned him to safeguard the faith: "In desiring to mitigate the severity of his punishment, you are acting the part of a friend to a man who is most hostile to you. But I beseech you so to manage the matter that no one at all may rashly dare to publish new dogmas and throw everything into confusion for such a long time as he has done."

The trial dragged on for months, with the Libertines, who now had the greater power in the city, trying to turn it to their own advantage and to discredit Calvin. But they had to walk warily. The case was not an easy one for them. They dared not champion such an extreme heretic as Servetus openly. All they could do was to delay matters as much as they were able. In the end, the Council appealed to other Swiss Churches for advice. They were at one in declaring Servetus a heretic. After this there could be no doubt of the outcome. On October 26, 1553, Servetus was condemned to be burned, Calvin's request that he might die more swiftly by the axe being refused. The following day sentence was executed.

This affair very properly shocks us. But while we condemn Calvin's actions, we ought in fairness to take his difficulties into account, and, what is more, to see why we are shocked. The difficulties are plain, and the Zürich ministers put their finger on the spot when they wrote to Calvin: "We think that in this case you ought to show great faith and zeal, inasmuch as our Churches have abroad the bad reputation of being heretical and of being particularly favorable to heresy."

According to Rome, the Protestant Churches were heretical in their doctrines of grace and the Church. If now they could say that they were also heretical on the doctrine of the Trinity and of the nature of Christ, they would have won a notable triumph which might have had serious results in the future. If Servetus had been tolerated in Geneva this is just what the Romanists would have claimed. Here was Calvin's dilemma.

What can we say but that he should never have fought the battle of faith with the world's weapons?

Moreover, what is it that so shocks us in this case? Not, surely, only that a man was burned to death, horrible though that is. It is that he was burned to death in the Reformed city of Geneva. At the time of the Reformation, literally hundreds of the Protestants were burned by the Romanists. We take it almost for granted, for Rome was a persecuting Church. It is because Calvin knew better that we are shocked. When a man of blameless respectability commits a crime and is sent to prison, we are far more horrified than when a dozen hardened criminals are convicted. So with Calvin and Rome. One burning less or more was neither here nor there to Rome, and it is a thousand pities they ever let Servetus escape; but this one burning has burnt an ineradicable scar on Calvin's reputation.

A month before Servetus' death, the Libertines, seeing they were unlikely to make much more capital out of this heretic, tried a different attack, this time on Calvin's main position. They thought themselves now strong enough to defy him openly and perhaps decisively. For this purpose a member of the old Genevan family of Berthelier was cast in the role of decoy. He had, some time before, been excommunicated by the Consistory. Now, at the instigation of his leaders, he applied to be admitted again to the Lord's Supper. But he made his application, not to the Consistory, but to the Council. Their permission was given, in the face of Calvin's repeated and vehement expostulation.

September 3 was Communion Sunday and the decisive day. If he admitted Berthelier to the Sacrament he would, in effect, be acknowledging the right of the state to order the life of the Church. Not only would he be defeated, but his work in Geneva and his example to other Protestant Churches overthrown. But he had not fought for so many years to see everything brought to nothing at the last. At that time, he was preaching on Sundays on the Acts of the Apostles. He spoke during his sermon of the wickedness of treating the Lord's Supper lightly or profanely. Then he raised his voice and his hand in that characteristic gesture of his and quoted Chrysostom: "I will die sooner than this hand shall stretch forth the sacred things of the Lord to those who have been judged despisers."

The atmosphere in the Cathedral, where, of course, everyone knew what was happening, was tense. Beza tells us that "the Sacrament was celebrated in an extraordinary silence, not without a certain fear and trembling, as if the Deity Himself had been present." In fact, however, the danger was already passed, since the nerves of the conspirators had cracked, and Berthelier had been warned not to present himself after all and was not even in the Cathedral.

In ignorance of this, Calvin expected exile, and that afternoon preached a farewell sermon. But, although the struggle was to continue for a whole year more, the Libertines had received their deathblow. The end came when, seeing that they had been defeated over the question of excommunication, they instigated a rising in the city against the French immigrants. The attempt broke before the courage and determination of Bonna, one of the Senate. It seems now as if there were noise and fury rather than deeds, but at the time the Council thought it was not simply a riot but an armed attempt to seize power. Their attitude was so threatening that Perrin and other leaders fled in fear to Berne, which, willing to sting Geneva, gave them ready welcome. In their absence they were condemned to death, a sentence which they escaped but which was executed on some lesser members of the party and also Berthelier, when he was foolish enough to return.

The opposition was now finally broken. For the rest of his life, Calvin held a position of great authority in the city, was deferred to by the Council, and became something of a Grand Old Man of the Reformed Church, even in Geneva.

But there was to be no resting for him. He could from here give all his energies, unhindered by the exhausting struggle, to his pastoral work, his preaching, teaching, and writing. When he came to die, he said with satisfaction that things were different from when he first came to Geneva. But this victory must not be conceived of as simply a victory for a church polity or a system of discipline, but as a victory of the Word of God. The Gospel was preached in Geneva, the Sacraments were administered, and the Church could strengthen both preaching and administration by her right to exercise discipline. The conflict with the Libertines was a fight for the purity and freedom of the Church. Nor should the outcome be misconceived. The Libertine party was overcome in battle and destroyed. But many citizens who had been unbelievers were brought by the same preaching into the kingdom of God.

The ten years remaining to Calvin after 1554 were not a despotic rule by the Church. The change in the city represented a genuine change in the lives of many citizens. Not everyone had been converted. Not everyone was peaceable or teachable. But a city that had been a byword for rioting and immorality of many kinds was now known as one of the godly cities of Europe. This was the real victory that was won.

# THE ECUMENICAL CHURCHMAN

## 1

"Of the true Church, with which we ought to keep unity because she is the mother of all the godly." These words are not the title of a Papal Encyclical but of the first chapter of Book IV of the *Institutes*. Whenever Calvin speaks of the Church, it is with this warmth. It will be remembered that herein lay one of the greatest stumbling blocks in the way of his joining the Reformers (if the passage in the *Letter to Cardinal Sadoleto* be, as it sounds, autobiographical):

> One thing in particular made me averse to these new teachers—reverence for the Church. But when once I opened my ears and allowed myself to be taught, I saw that this fear of derogating from the majesty of the Church was groundless. For they reminded me how great is the difference between schism from the Church and studying to correct the faults by which the Church herself was contaminated. They spoke nobly of the Church and showed the greatest desire to cultivate unity.

Luther and Calvin were no firebrand revolutionaries, but responsible men who saw around them a Church which made a mockery of the New Testament picture of the Church. They dared not, having God as their Judge, draw back from the task to which they were impelled of calling the Church to reform herself in accordance with the Scriptures. If the Church had heeded their voices there would have been no split into Roman Catholic and Protestant Churches. But if the Church refused to hear, what then? What was Luther to do? He believed with all his heart that the Roman Church had fallen away from the gospel of Christ. If he obeyed the Papal summons to recant, where would be his obedience to the command of Christ to preach that gospel? With John Hus he followed the apostles' dictum that it is better to obey God than men, and stood firm—"Here I stand; I can do no other." But when he had been excommunicated by what he now held to be an erring and false Church, how was it possible to avoid setting up "another" Church?

Short of Luther recanting or Rome reforming its doctrine as radically as a little later it changed its way of life, it is impossible to see how the existence of a Protestant Church alongside the Roman Church could have been avoided. Looking back, Calvin applauds Luther's stand, perceiving clearly his early moderation and the situation he was placed in by the Roman refusal of his cry for reform:

> When Luther first came forward, he merely touched with a gentle hand a few abuses of the grossest description, now grown intolerable. And he did it with a modesty which suggested that he had more desire to see them corrected than determination to correct them himself. The opposite party forthwith sounded to arms; and when the contention got more and more inflamed our enemies deemed it the best and shortest method to suppress the truth by cruelty and violence.

And again: "Any man who considers how Luther and the other reformers acted at the beginning and how they afterwards proceeded will deem it unnecessary to call upon us for any defense."

By the time Calvin came on the scene Luther's excommunication was fifteen years past, and the Protestant Churches, despite recurrent fears that they might be trampled out of existence in the turmoil of European politics, were firmly established. Occasionally conferences were held to try to reach, if not agreement, at least a *modus vivendi* with Rome, but they inevitably broke down by the time the Eucharist was discussed. Some Reformers, and notably Philip Melanchthon, were willing to go a long way to reach agreement, even to step beyond the boundaries of what they believed. Calvin, prizing truth above even unity, would have none of this.

There was that time at Ratisbon in 1541 when agreement seemed so close. For the Protestants appeared Bucer, Melanchthon, and the obscure Pistorius; among the Romanists was Luther's fierce adversary of earlier days, Eck, but the other two were of a quieter spirit. The Romanists were ready to allow priests to marry and for the laity to receive both bread and wine at the Communion. The two sides even managed to agree on justification. Then, in spite of Melanchthon's and Bucer's contortions of compromise, the conference shipwrecked on the doctrine of the Eucharist. Calvin, present as an advisor, wrote and told Farel what he thought of it all:

> So far as I can understand, if we could be content with only a half Christ we might easily come to understand one another. Philip and Bucer have drawn up ambiguous and insincere formulas on transubstantiation, to see if they could satisfy the opposite party while conceding nothing. I could not agree to this device, although they think they have reasonable grounds for doing it. For they hope that in a little while they might begin to see more clearly if the matter of doctrine be left open for the present. So they want to skip it, and are not afraid of that equivocation in matters of conscience than which nothing can possibly be more hurtful.

The heart of the matter for him comes in this quotation: whether they should have a half Christ or the fullness of Christ—whether they should worship and follow the Christ of the Scriptures alone, basing their whole life as a Church and as individuals upon Him, or whether they should build only partly upon Christ and partly also upon some other foundation.

The gravamen of his quarrel with Rome was not the moral laxity of the Vatican or the priesthood or the monasteries, not even such abuses as the withholding of the cup from the laity or private masses. It was that Rome had destroyed the glory of Christ in many ways—by calling upon the saints to intercede, when Jesus Christ is the one Mediator between God and man; by adoring the Blessed Virgin, when Christ alone shall be adored; by offering a continual sacrifice in the Mass, when the sacrifice of Christ upon the Cross is complete and sufficient. Calvin will make it quite clear in the *Commentary on Galatians* that he considers the Romanists outside Christ: "the Papists, choosing to have a divided and mangled Christ, have no Christ at all, and are therefore 'removed from Christ.' They are full of superstitions which are directly at variance with the nature of Christ. Let it be carefully observed, then, that we are 'removed from Christ' when we fall into those views which are inconsistent with His mediatorial office." Time after time, he will return to this point. In the *Institutes*, he will say bluntly:

"It was necessary for us to withdraw from them in order to approach to Christ."

The glory of Christ is the theme that runs through the treatise on *The Necessity for Reforming the Church* which Calvin addressed to the Emperor Charles V: "Let our opponents, then, first of all draw near to Christ and afterwards let them accuse us of schism in daring to dissent from them in doctrine. But, since I have made it plain that Christ is banished from their society and the teaching of His gospel exterminated, their charge against us simply amounts to this, that we cleave to Christ rather than to them."

Not that Calvin had no desire for unity among the Churches. His love of peace and reverence for the wholeness of the Church impelled him to seek agreement—but not at the price of the gospel: "Peace is indeed to be longed for and sought with the utmost zeal; but rather than that it should be purchased by any loss of godliness, let heaven and earth, if need be, go into confusion." There was to be no peace between the Roman and the Protestant Churches. Each had set out on its long path into the centuries, gradually diverging further from the other. Assuredly Calvin is right; the one place where the Churches can meet, find agreement, and become one will be in the whole Christ.

## 2

The original split from the Roman Church was, in face of its refusal to reform, inevitable. The divisions within the Protestants ranks, however, were a different matter. In a sense the antagonism between Lutheran and Zwinglian was only the recognition of a fact latent from the beginning, for two strands had been present in the Reformation all along. Zwingli always insisted that he had reached his understanding of the gospel independently of Luther and at about the same time. However that may be, his outlook was very different and, as leader of the early Swiss Reformation, he impressed his outlook upon his followers. He had been profoundly influenced by the humanists and owed less to the schoolmen than did Luther, and this clean break with the immediate past gave him a far more radical attitude than Luther could stomach.

Relations between them were soon strained, but they met at Marburg in 1529 in an attempt to come to terms. They agreed on everything—except the Eucharist. And here both were immovable. In the end, despite their substantial agreement, the conference only served to magnify the differences and bring it into the foreground.

It is a great pity that Calvin and Luther never met, or that Calvin had not been born a few years earlier, before Luther had hardened his attitude. They were far closer to one another both theologically and in spirit than Luther and Zwingli had been. But their only real contact was through common friends. Calvin is delighted when he hears that Bucer has had a letter from Luther saying, "Salute John Sturm and John Calvin, whose books I have read with particular pleasure," and Melanchthon tells him, "Luther and Pomeranus have desired Calvin to be greeted; Calvin has acquired great favor in their eyes." When some loving souls sought to stir up trouble between them by pointing out a passage in Calvin's book on the Lord's Supper where he criticizes Luther, the German Reformer said with unaccustomed gentleness: "I hope that Calvin will one day think better of us; but in any case, it is well that even now he should have a proof of our good feeling towards him." "If we are not moved by such moderation, we are certainly made of stone," says Calvin to Farel. "For myself, I am profoundly moved by it."

But the acquaintance made no progress into friendship. They passed only within hailing distance of each other. Four years later, Calvin was still no further forward than asking Melanchthon to "salute Doctor Martin respectfully in my name." Luther's last years were clouded by trouble and overwork, his temper dangerous and uncertain. More and more he became inflamed against the Zürich theologians, the successors of Zwingli, who retaliated in like. Farel begged Calvin to use his moderating influence to calm down the men of Zürich. He replied that the real trouble now was Luther, whom Bullinger had borne with meekly and patiently for long. But nevertheless, he wrote to Bullinger soon after, enjoining moderation:

> I hear that Luther has at last broken out in fierce invective, not so much against you as against the whole of us.
> . . . But I do most seriously want to ask you to consider how eminent a man Luther is, and the excellent endowments he is gifted with, his strength of mind and resolute constancy, with what great skill and efficiency and power of doctrinal statement he has hitherto devoted his whole energy to overthrowing the reign of anti-Christ, and at the same time to diffusing far and near the doctrine of salvation. I have often been accustomed to declare that

even though he were to call me a devil, I should none the less still hold him in such honor that I must acknowledge him to be an illustrious servant of God. But, while he is endued with rare and excellent virtues, he labors at the same time under serious faults. Would that he had rather studied to curb this restless, uneasy temperament which is so apt to boil over in every direction. . . . Besides, you will do yourselves no good by quarrelling, but will only afford some sport to the wicked, so that they may triumph, not so much over us as over the gospel. . . . Even should he have provoked us, we ought to decline the contest rather than increase the harm by the general shipwreck of the Church.

Even more important, he wrote to Luther himself a most reverent letter, calling him "my much respected father," and sending two or three of his smaller books. Melanchthon, to whom he entrusted the letter, refused to pass it on; Luther, he said, was too suspicious of the Swiss Reformers. But there was certainly nothing in it to arouse even Luther's wrath. On the contrary, it was conciliatory in the extreme. It included:

Would that I might fly to you that I might even for a few hours enjoy the happiness of your company. For I would prefer, and it would be far better, not only upon this ques-tion, but also upon others, to talk to you personally. But seeing that is not granted to us on earth, I hope that it will shortly come to pass in the kingdom of God. Adieu, most renowned sir, most distinguished minister of Christ and my ever honored father.

But his chief contacts with the Lutheran Church were through Melanch-thon and Bucer, both his close friends. Melanchthon was, in nearly all respects, a man after Calvin's own heart. A mighty scholar—professor of Greek at Wittenberg at the age of twenty-one—a humanist of wide sym-pathies and a Reformer who had the care of all the Churches at heart.

His trouble was that, unlike Calvin, he never overcame his reserve and timidity. There was more than one complaint that he, who could write and talk so well of the Cross, had not learned to live under the Cross.

And this was to be a hindrance, not only in leading to overmuch accommodation (for accommodation never yet brought about lasting union), but also in helping to prevent the important conference of all the Reformed Churches. But the friendship between him and Calvin served to bring about at least a closer understanding between the two Churches. They were to fail in the end before the obstinacy of the second generation of Lutheran theologians who, entrenching themselves firmly in Luther's theology, called Melanchthon a crypto-Calvinist and refused concessions, far less unity. After the Peace of Augsburg, when the Lutheran Church was granted the same rights as the Roman Church in Germany, there was even less chance of agreement. In the future, there was to be a shrewish bitterness between Lutheran and Reformed that, in earlier days, had been reserved for the common enemy, Rome.

3

In Switzerland, also, unity had to be fought for. There the situation was more confused than in Germany. The politically independent towns and cantons were free to choose their own religion. Part of the country clave still to the Roman Church, and even among the Reformed cities there was wide diversity. Zürich was dominated by Zwingli and afterwards by his disciple Bullinger. Berne tended to Lutheranism. And Basel, under the influence of Martin Bucer, tried to tread the slippery *via media* between Luther and Zwingli. What was worse, the diversities of doctrine, worship, and organization were exacerbated by centuries-old feuds and jealousies between towns and families.

From the outset, Calvin aimed at bringing the Swiss Churches to unity. As early as 1538, he was writing to Bullinger:

> Oh, if only a pure and sincere agreement could be reached among us at last! What then would prevent the assembling of a public synod, where individuals might propose whatever they may think to be best for the Churches? A way might be found out of going to work by common deliberation, and, if need be, that the cities and princes also should assist in this undertaking by mutual exhortation and counsel, and also confirm what is done by their authority. But in so great perplexity, the Lord is rather to

be inquired of, that He Himself may open up the way.

Little progress was made, and the Churches remained like so many stooks of corn in a harvest field before they are gathered into one rick, similar but separate. However, the leaders continued in friendliness, despite some provocation from Zürich against Bucer, generally distrusted as a mediator.

Now, as later in regard to Luther, Calvin wrote to Bullinger and pleaded for moderation and a friendly spirit. When Bucer is at fault, he says, tell him so, and he will take it in the right way. But do it, not as if you were enemies, but with the love that there ought to be between fellow-ministers of Christ. And again he returns to the hope of unity:

> What, dear Bullinger, ought we rather to correspond about at this time than the preserving and confirming, by every means in our power, brotherly kindness among our-selves? We see, indeed, of how much importance it is, not only on our own account, but for the sake of the whole body of professing Christians everywhere, that all those on whom the Lord has laid any personal charge in the ordering of His Church should agree together in a sincere and cordial understanding. . . . Since, therefore, it is our duty carefully to cultivate friendly fellowship with all the ministers of Christ, so we must needs also endeavor by all the means we can to see that the Churches to which we faithfully minister the Word of the Lord may agree among themselves.

Just as between Zwingli and Luther, so also between Zwingli's successors and Calvin and Bucer, it was the doctrine of the Lord's Supper that was the main point of disagreement. Bullinger was highly suspicious of Calvin as being more than half a Lutheran, and apparently nothing Calvin could say or do would make him change his mind—"a preconceived opinion of me leads you to imagine and attribute to me what never occurred to my mind." Besides, he was a friend of Bucer's, and that in itself was sufficient to damn him. The squalid bickerings went on and on alongside the wholehearted agreements, marring what Calvin called "the springtime of a reviving Church." It was not until 1549 that his patience had its reward with the union of all the Swiss Reformed Churches when they subscribed to the Consensus of Zürich which he and Bullinger had drawn up. This was a solid achievement to offset the disagreement with the Lutherans. From here on there was one Reformed Church in Switzerland.

<h1 style="text-align:center">4</h1>

Calvin was not the first nor by any means the last Continental theologian to misunderstand the English religious situation. It was not entirely surprising, for he had never visited England, knew no English, and often relied for his information upon men of inferior judgment or who were too far from the center of events to perceive their intricacies or significance. For example, his censure of the 1552 Book of Common Prayer—the book that was too Protestant for England!—largely sprang from his incomplete knowledge of the background, as also from the immoral way it was presented to him by the English Puritan refugees at Frankfort: "In the Anglican liturgy," he replied to them, "as you describe it to me, I see that many things are pretty inept." The loyal Anglicans at Frankfort were deeply hurt, wrote in expostulation, and had little difficulty in rebutting the charges that the Puritans had made against their book.

Nevertheless, he had maintained his interest in England from quite early days until his death. Cranmer and he wrote polite letters to each other, never heartily cordial as with Melanchthon or Bucer, but yet friendly enough. He dedicated his *Commentary on Isaiah* to the young king Edward VI, "a truly Christian prince," and some years later its second edition to Queen Elizabeth. At the end of the fifteen-forties, he had great hopes of the Protector Somerset, and wrote to him letters that are almost long enough to be called treatises, on the best way of reforming the English Church. Such letters to those in high places should not be seen as an uncalled-for interference. Rather, he is writing in the succession of St. Bernard of Clairvaux, who, himself but an abbot, told kings and popes their duty without mincing his words but with the perfect courtesy of humility. His words to Pope Innocent II would serve as a motto to some of Calvin's letters: "Boldly I speak, because faithfully I love."

The Duke of Somerset had become Protector of England on the accession of Edward VI in January 1547. Calvin had heard favorable reports of him and began a correspondence with him in 1548 when he dedicated the *Commentary on Timothy* to him. In his first letter, he pressed for a complete reformation of the Church—and this, he says, means three things: the sound instruction of the people, the rooting out of abuses, and the repression and correction of vice. This first letter led also to favor with the King. Francis Burgoyne, formerly one of Calvin's secretaries, wrote to him from London: "Our Josiah, the king of England, made most courteous inquiry of me concerning your health and ministry. To which when I had made such reply as in my judgment I considered worthy of you, he declared plainly enough both by his countenance and his words that he takes a great interest in you and in everything concerning you."

When the cataclysm of Mary's reign overwhelmed the English Church, Calvin was filled with dismay. In great sorry and anxiety, he wrote to Beza:

> This English affair has distressed me almost more than anything else. Let us earnestly implore mercy of God, that He may have pity upon us and upon His most afflicted Church. But where is our Peter Martyr? Where is John a Lasco? Where is Hooper, Bishop of Worcester? Where is Cranmer, Archbishop of Canterbury? Where is the Duke of Suffolk? Where are numberless other excellent men? Lord, have mercy upon them! I cannot easily express how greatly these things distress me.

He was soon able to give practical evidence of his concern by caring for English refugees, and Number Eleven, Rue des Chanoines became a sort of sixteenth-century Bishop of Chichester's palace to many of them. Sir Richard Moryson, "the merry knight" and former English ambassador to the Emperor, spoke for the rest when he thanked him "that you have given up to us your house, and become a mere tenant in your own home."

Elizabeth's reign began inauspiciously for Calvin. Great as was his influence through the returning refugees (so that the Romanist Bishop White of Winchester, preaching at Queen Mary's funeral, was led to speak words of warning: "At this present, I warn you, the wolves be coming out of Geneva, and other places of Germany, and have sent their books before, full of pestilent doctrines, blasphemy and heresy, to infect the people"), yet he failed to win the friendship of either Elizabeth or her right hand, William Cecil. It was John Knox's fault, in fact, for while he was living in Geneva in Queen Mary's time, he published a book denying women the right to reign and bearing the resounding title *The first blast of the trumpet against the monstrous regiment and empire of women.* Since it was published in Geneva, Calvin himself was blamed as if he had approved it.

When, therefore, a messenger delivered the second edition of the *Commentary on Isaiah* to Elizabeth, to whom it was dedicated, she did not receive it kindly. Moreover, Cecil said some things to the messenger which, Calvin suggested, "seem to me more severe than was consistent with your courtesy." He wrote to Cecil, stating his own views and protesting that he had no part in Knox's book and was annoyed when he first heard of it a year after publication. But the future brought little good will, and Calvin became unfortunately the property, almost exclusively, of the English Puritans. Knox, that Scottish Farel, had done more harm than he could have imagined.

5

But it was France that remained his especial care. An international theologian and churchman he might be, but in Germany, England, even Switzerland, he was a foreigner. In France he was on his own soil. Though he was forced to leave France, he continued to exercise his ministry there through his letters and books. The French Protestants, for their part, looked up to him not only as their chief pastor but as a father. When he writes to them, a particular note of affection creeps into his letters.

His work for France can only be compared, in intensity and also in method, with the foreign missionary movement of the eighteenth and nineteenth centuries. From his base in Geneva, he maintained a supply, not only of French Bibles and Reformed literature, but also of colporteurs and pastors. Between 1555 and 1564, over a hundred pastors were sent. Churches sprang up in Meaux and Paris, Orleans and Rouen, Bordeaux, Toulouse, and a dozen other towns. In 1558, Calvin said it was reckoned that there were three hundred thousand Protestants in this officially Roman Catholic country. Throughout the country, groups of Protestants assembled for their worship, if need be in secret. Some of them enjoyed the ministry of pastors, and those who had none would read the Scriptures and the sermons that had been preached in St. Pierre and faithfully taken down by Denis Raguenier. Under Calvin's guidance, the groups came together into one Church, organized according to the pattern in the *Institutes*—so that it was in France, and not in Geneva, that his concept of the Church was realized. He seized every opportunity that offered of winning toleration for the French Reformed Church from the government. Once he undertook a journey through Switzerland, visiting Berne, Zürich, Schaffhausen, Basel and, Strassburg to canvass support for these persecuted Christians.

Nowhere are his care for France and his love for the persecuted more evident than in the story of the five prisoners of Lyons. Five young Frenchmen had been trained as pastors in Lausanne, from where, in 1552, they journey into France. Almost immediately they were arrested and were imprisoned in Lyons. Soon after, Calvin wrote to them:

> As soon as you were taken, we heard of it, and knew how it had come to pass. We took care that help might be sent you with all speed, and are now awaiting the result. Those who have influence with the prince in whose power has God put your lives, are faithfully exerting themselves on your behalf, but we do not yet know how far they have succeeded in their suit. Meanwhile all the children of God pray for you as they are bound to do, not only on account of the mutual compassion which ought to exist between members of the same body, but because they know well that you labor for them by maintaining the cause of their salvation. We hope, come what may, that God will give a happy issue to your captivity, so that we shall have reason to rejoice.

After a prolonged trial and in spite of all that the Swiss Churches could do for them, they were condemned to death by burning. Calvin at once wrote off to them:

> We who are here shall do our duty in praying that He would glorify Himself more and more by your constancy, and that He may, by the comfort of His Spirit, sweeten and endear all that is bitter to the flesh, and so absorb your spirits in Himself, that in contemplating that heavenly crown, you may be ready without regret to leave all that belongs to this world. . . . And now, my brethren, after having besought our good Lord to have charge over you, to assist you in everything and through everything, to make you taste by experience how kind a Father He is, and how careful of the salvation of His own, I beg to be remembered in your prayers.

The next month saw further desperate efforts on their behalf. Berne appealed to the King of France. But in vain. They were to die. On April 22, 1553, Calvin told Viret that no hope was left. To them he wrote a farewell letter:

> Now, at this present hour, necessity itself exhorts you more than ever to turn your whole mind heavenward. As yet, we know not what will be the event. But since it appears as though God would use your blood to seal His truth, there is nothing better for you than to prepare yourselves for that end, beseeching Him so to subdue you to His good pleasure, that nothing may hinder you from following whithersoever He shall call. . . . Since it pleases Him to employ you to the death in maintaining His quarrel, He will strengthen your hands in the fight and will not suffer a single drop of your blood to be shed in vain.

And the greatest theologian since Aquinas, the prince of the Church who writes boldly to kings and princes, signs himself, "Your humble brother, John Calvin." He is humble, for they are doing what he was not called upon to do, sealing their testimony with their blood; but he is their brother, for, as it has been said, "Among the martyrs, with whom Calvin constantly conversed in spirit, he became a martyr himself; he lived and felt like a man before whom the whole earth disappears."

\* \* \*

Switzerland, Germany, England, France, Poland also, Italy, and the Netherlands—to all these countries Calvin spoke with an almost apostolic voice. They might not always like what he had to say, but they paid heed to his opinion. He had accomplished much for the Churches. In Switzerland and France, the Protestant Churches were united. But the greatest prize of all eluded his grasp. The union of all the Churches of the Reformation which he, with Cranmer, so greatly desired, was not to be.

The great Protestant Council was once so close, provoked by the convening of the Council of Trent. Bullinger had written to Cranmer, urging that England should not send a delegate to the Council of Trent. He replied that the King had never thought of doing so, but added that he had recommended that "His Majesty grant his assistance, that in England, or elsewhere, there might be convoked a synod of the most learned and excellent persons, in which provision might be made for the purity of Church doctrine, and especially for an agreement upon the sacramentarian controversy." On the same day he wrote in similar terms to Calvin, who replied that he would cross ten seas to attend such a council.

But when Cranmer invited Melanchthon, the scheme shipwrecked, for his fear of the long journey was augmented when he consulted the stars, of which he was a hopeful student. The Reformed Churches stayed apart, and Calvin's desire has yet to be fulfilled: "Would that the union between all Christ's Churches upon earth were such, that the angels in heaven might join their song of praise."

He had travelled a far distance from those early days—the little boy telling over his Latin grammar under the shadow of Noyon Cathedral; the theology student grasping subtleties as elusive as the motes in the sunbeams in the dusty classrooms of Paris; the well-dressed young man distilling his precious sentences; the scholar seeking his ivory tower and finding Geneva; the passionate reformer forgetting his fear of men in his travail for the Word of God; the statesman and the counselor of the Churches.

He had been an old man for many years, and they said at the end that when you met him in the street it was like seeing a corpse walking, so emaciated was he with his many ailments and diseases. On his deathbed, "nothing seemed left but his spirit," said Beza.

When he had died, all Geneva desired to see his body, as if he were a medieval saint or one of those relics that he had so sardonically mocked. But he had seen to it that there should be no posthumous canonization and left orders that he should be buried in an unmarked grave. Thus his death and burial were of one piece with his life; as a good witness, he would not be regarded, but bent all his energies in life and death to making Jesus Christ alone great, and making that greatness visible.

We misunderstand him and the meaning of his life if we would make of him a hero, whether striking blows for freedom—

> *those great captains of reform,*
> *Luther and Calvin; who, whate'er they taught,*
> *Led folk from superstition to free thought—*

or even as the leader of a great religious crusade. He has his place in history, of course, and an honorable place at that. But in the account of the history of faith, his words and his life point from himself to where the crucified and risen Christ sits at the right hand of God. We may leave this man where he lies in his unknown grave and hear simply his voice, not as the tired whisper of a ghost over the years, but with all the power that once stirred St. Pierre, glorifying God and His Son.

# ❊❊ desiringGod

If you would like to further explore the vision of God and life presented in this book, we at Desiring God would love to serve you. We have hundreds of resources to help you grow in your passion for Jesus Christ and help you spread that passion to others. At our website, desiringGod.org, you'll find almost everything John Piper has written and preached, including more than thirty books. We've made over twenty-five years of his sermons available free online for you to read, listen to, download, and in some cases watch.

In addition, you can access hundreds of articles, find out where John Piper is speaking, learn about our conferences, discover our God-centered children's curricula, and browse our online store. John Piper receives no royalties from the books he writes and no compensation from Desiring God. The funds are all reinvested into our gospel-spreading efforts. Desiring God also has a whatever-you-can-afford policy, designed for individuals with limited discretionary funds. If you'd like more information about this policy, please contact us at the address or phone number below. We exist to help you treasure Jesus Christ and his gospel above all things because he is most glorified in you when you are most satisfied in him. Let us know how we can serve you!

**Desiring God**
Post Office Box 2901 Minneapolis, Minnesota 55402
888.346.4700 mail@desiringGod.org